D0899364

INFLUENTIAL LEADERSHIP

INFLUENTIAL LEADERSHIP
Change Your Behavior,
Change Your Organization,
Change Health Care

Michael E. Frisina

HEALTH FORUM, INC.
An American Hospital Association Company
Chicago

Printed in the United States of America

ISBN: 978-1-55648-382-0   Item Number: 088710

PROJECT MANAGER: Joyce Dunne
EDITORIAL ASSISTANT: Barbara Novosel
LAYOUT AND TYPESETTING: Fine Print, Ltd.
COVER DESIGN: Cheri Kusek
PRODUCTION MANAGER: Martin Weitzel
ACQUISITIONS AND DEVELOPMENT: Richard Hill

Library of Congress Cataloging-in-Publication Data

Frisina, Michael E.
   Influential leadership : change your behavior, change your organization, change health care / Michael E. Frisina.
     p. cm.
   ISBN 978-1-55648-382-0 (alk. paper)
1. Health services administrators. 2. Leadership. I. Title.
   RA971.F746 2011
   362.1068–dc22
                                                        2011001244

This book is dedicated to my father, Anthony Alphonse Frisina. He was a first-generation Italian American who lived as a young teen through the Great Depression and volunteered to serve in the United States Marine Corps during the Second World War. Born in a very small town in northwest Pennsylvania, he taught me the virtues of discipline, hard work, and fidelity. For many of his generation, his war experiences shaped much of what he believed and how he behaved the rest of his life. Consequently, as his only son, I was shaped and molded by them as well. A member of the 1st Marine Division and a survivor of the Battle of Guadalcanal, he was, first, foremost, and forever, a United States Marine.

Semper Fidelis (Always Faithful): These words were not a mere slogan to my father, nor have they been for countless United States Marines who served before and after him in the rich tradition of "The Corps." They represent an absolute and embody a culture—a collection of beliefs and behaviors—that are not negotiable, any time, under any circumstances. I was raised in the context of this cultural norm, and I was expected to live by it, in my character and behavior, with integrity and through the pursuit of excellence. I may not always have been the best at what I attempted to do, but I was always required to give my best effort to the last fiber of my mind, body, and spirit.

I pray you take the meaning and spirit of *semper fidelis* with you into your life as an added blessing for having read this book.

Contents

List of Figures ix

About the Author xi

Acknowledgments xiii

Introduction to Influential Leadership 1

PART **I**   **What Is Self-Awareness?** 15

CHAPTER 1   Self-Awareness: The Basic Competency
             of the Influential Leader. 17

CHAPTER 2   The Volitional and Mental Dimensions 39

CHAPTER 3   The Emotional Dimension 59

PART **II**   **What Is Collaboration?** 83

CHAPTER 4   Collaboration: The Duty of the
             Influential Leader. 87

CHAPTER 5   Trust: The Heart of Collaboration. 115

CHAPTER 6   Accountability: The Soul of Collaboration. . . . 135

PART **III**   **What Is Connection?** 157

CHAPTER 7   Connection: The Strategy of the
             Influential Leader. 159

CHAPTER 8   Leadership Behaviors That Hinder
             Connection. 181

Epilogue. 195

Suggested Readings. 199

Index 203

List of Figures

0-1   Fundamental Principles of Influential Leadership. 3

1-1   Influential Leadership and the Components
of the C^4 Model. 29

2-1   Living by Conviction: An Example 40

2-2   Sense of Urgency: An Example 44

2-3   Try This: Evaluate Your Mental Model 47

3-1   Seven Emotions-Based Employee Needs 68

3-2   Try This: Assess the Level of Engagement
in Your Organization 71

3-3   Emotional Awareness Questionnaire 72

4-1   Try This: Five Don'ts of Collaborative
Communication. 93

5-1   Try This: Assess the Trust Levels in Your Team 121

6-1   Try This: Assess Your Team's Collaboration and
Accountability 148

6-2   Sample Behavior-Standard Evaluation Form 150

7-1   Try This: Determine the Quality of Your
Connections. 161

7-2   Try This: Connect with Others on an Emotional
Level 169

7-3   The Principles of Focusing on People. 175

8-1   Try This: Simple Ways to Invite Connections
and Maintain Good Behavior 190

About the Author

Michael E. Frisina, PhD, is an author, an educator, and a consultant specializing in health care leadership and performance improvement. After holding leadership positions at Providence Hospital and the Providence Heart and Vascular Institute, Columbia, South Carolina, and at the Tuomey Healthcare System, Sumter, South Carolina, for more than fourteen years, Dr. Frisina founded The Frisina Group, a leadership consulting and teaching consortium based in Columbia, South Carolina. The Frisina Group specializes in leader development, performance coaching, and organizational development, focusing its training on key methodologies for providing safe, high-quality, and patient-centered care.

In 2007 Dr. Frisina was selected as the Area Health Education Consortium Educator of the Year for South Carolina. Before entering civilian health care, Dr. Frisina served as a lieutenant colonel in the U.S. Army, where he held a variety of positions of increasing responsibility—including consultant to the army surgeon general for medical research and development, consultant to the Department of Defense Human Genome Project, and executive officer at Tripler Army Medical Center, Honolulu. Lieutenant Colonel Frisina also served as a faculty member and subject matter expert in leadership and ethics at the United States Military Academy at West Point, New York; the Uniformed Services University of Health Sciences and School of Medicine, Bethesda, Maryland; and the United States Army Academy of Health Sciences, San Antonio, Texas.

Dr. Frisina received his BS degree with honors from Saint Bonaventure University, graduating as a distinguished military graduate. He earned his MA degree and completed doctoral course work at Indiana University, later receiving his doctorate, magna cum laude, from the University of Auberdeen. He completed postgraduate studies at the University of Cambridge, earning a certificate in international bioethics from Girton College.

A certified expert in continuous quality improvement methodologies, Dr. Frisina is featured in *Doing the Right Things Right,* a prestigious publication of demonstrated best-practice hospitals published by The Joint Commission. He has been a visiting fellow in Medical Humanities at the Medical College of Pennsylvania and a visiting scholar at The Hastings Center. In addition, he has presented at the American Hospital Association and Health Forum Leadership Summit and continues to serve on the Health Forum faculty. He has authored numerous papers and published several articles on leadership and organizational effectiveness. He is a contributing author to the Borden Institute's highly acclaimed textbook series on military medicine.

Among his various military awards and decorations, Dr. Frisina is a recipient of the coveted Order of Military Medical Merit for lifetime achievement and contributions to the U.S. Army Medical Department, as well as the U.S. Army Legion of Merit.

Acknowledgments

The success of any important project is the result of superior team effort. No one wins alone. I would be violating the principles and the purpose of this book if I did not give adequate praise to the many people who helped me complete what I believe to be a very important contribution to increasing the level of organizational performance.

My sincere and heartfelt thanks go to my wife of thirty-one years, Susan. Her honesty and candor have kept me grounded, and she challenges me to live a life of integrity every day.

To my children, Michael, Robert, and Rebekah, who remind me continually that to fail to practice what I teach has rippling effects into their lives and the lives of other people. I am so proud to be your father.

To Jane Calayag and Joyce Dunne, whose expert guidance has helped me to realize my vision for this book and to bring it to its final form.

And finally, to the AHA Press team at Health Forum: Pat Foy, Mary Grayson, Rick Hill, Cheri Kusek, Jeri Luga, Barbara Novosel, Sandy Rebitzer, Katie Sroka, and Marty Weitzel. Thank you for providing me this opportunity to share my passion for leadership excellence. I so appreciate your dedication and commitment to excellence as you live the credo of this book in your own organizational culture and individual behaviors.

To all of you I graciously extend my enduring gratitude and God's blessings.

INFLUENTIAL LEADERSHIP

Introduction
to Influential Leadership

The hardest thing is not to get people to accept new ideas;
it is to get them to forget old ones.

—John Maynard Keynes, economist

You have heard the saying "Some people make things happen. Other people watch what happens. Still others wonder what happened." Leadership, in general, is about making things happen. Influential leadership goes a step farther: It makes a positive difference in organizations and in the lives of people who serve and are served by that organization.

Influential leaders perform at a higher level, are more productive, and achieve greater results than other leaders faced with similar circumstances and given the same resources. The success and effectiveness of influential leaders are driven by a set of behaviors that enables them to become role models for followers, guide operational improvements, and sustain excellence.

A study of management and leadership literature, along with my observations of health care leaders with whom I have worked, reveals a common set of behaviors shared by highly successful leaders, regardless of gender, ethnic group, vocation, generation, or location. These behaviors fall under three categories: self-awareness, collaboration, and connection. They can be learned, but they must be practiced daily for them to yield the desired results. In other words, leaders must be willing to apply the behaviors to become influential and, by extension, effective and transformational.

A universal truth in high-performing organizations is that individual breakthroughs drive organizational breakthroughs.

This book is a means to this end, providing critical concepts in achieving organizational excellence and inspiring better performance.

Three Fundamental Principles of Influential Leadership

I have filled multiple leadership positions in my career—from brigade commander of my college's ROTC (Reserve Officers' Training Corps) military detachment to faculty member at the United States Military Academy at West Point to founder and chief executive officer of both for-profit and not-for-profit organizations. These experiences and my consulting work with various health care leaders have revealed one constant: Organizations that blossom and flourish are blessed with leaders who have not only the understanding of the fundamental principles of influential leadership (self-awareness, collaboration, and connection) but also the discipline to intentionally and purposefully apply the behaviors associated with these principles. (See figure 0-1.)

In contrast, organizations that lack this kind of leadership flounder in performance by accepting marginal success or living by the "good enough" cultural credo. These institutions are held back by leaders who are not self-aware, collaborative, or connective and thus are unable to inspire, develop, or implement performance breakthroughs that make a sustainable difference in the lives of people and the operations of the organization.

Self-Awareness: The Basic Competency of Influential Leaders

Think about all the people who have had leadership responsibility and authority over you. Who inspired, believed in, and encouraged you? When I reflect on this question, several teachers—from grade school to graduate school—come to mind. These teachers pushed me to try things I did not think I was capable of doing, supporting and mentoring me along the way.

Figure 0-1. Fundamental Principles of Influential Leadership

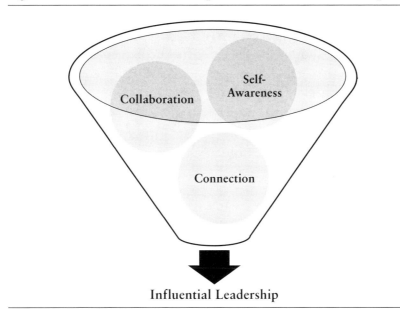

Influential Leadership

Now think about the people whose behaviors had a negative impact on you and your leadership development. Unfortunately, for many of us, this list includes so-called leaders, whose actions and words serve as an example of what we *do not* want to be like as a leader. One such leader from my past once made this comment: "Just remember I will always get all the credit, and you will always get all the blame." I will never forget that statement and its destructive effect on my motivation and morale.

This simple exercise emphasizes the impact that people in leadership positions have and the importance of self-awareness. Influential leaders are kind, considerate, honest, respectful, and trustworthy, among many other inspiring traits. Sadly, far too many leaders are the exact opposite, and they are unaware of how they are perceived by their peers and subordinates. As a result, they do not realize that their negative behavior contributes to lack of trust, loss of credibility, and the high cost of poor performance and low productivity. Worse, some leaders intentionally behave badly and are protective of those negative traits, believing at the least that they cause no harm.

By learning about the self, leaders become comfortable with their internal thought processes, values, beliefs, preferences, and emotions. They become self-managers, careful about how they present themselves and respond to the outside world. A self-aware leader, then, is in a better position to collaborate and connect with others, unlike a leader who is unaware of her true self.

Collaboration: The Duty of Influential Leaders

Leadership, at its core, is about getting a group of people to accomplish something that one person cannot do alone. Influential leaders rely on the principle of collaboration, knowing that people, not processes, strengthen or weaken the organization's pursuit of performance excellence. Specifically, these leaders rely on good behaviors—trust and accountability—to form a collaboration and move the organization toward its goals. A true collaboration is characterized by effective communication, cooperative attitudes, and integrated teams; these traits differentiate a collaboration from just any grouping of people assigned to complete a task.

Connection: The Strategy of Influential Leaders

When people are emotionally disconnected from their leaders, they are emotionally disconnected from their work and its accomplishment. As a result, performance suffers, productivity drops, and people withhold discretionary effort necessary to achieve at a high level. Influential leaders understand this dynamic and thus form bonds with those around them. They are charismatic, empathetic, compassionate, and approachable, traits that signal to others that they welcome and value a true connection with people.

The Performance Gap

Performance can be illustrated by this simple formula:

$$p = \text{technical skill} \times \text{motivation}$$

That is, performance (p) is the product of what we are *capable of doing* (technical skill) multiplied by what we are *willing to do* (motivation). In health care delivery, as in other high-risk industries, a gap between these two elements of performance can result in poor work quality that causes harm, suffering, and even a threat to human life.

Influential leaders are aware of these dire consequences. They hold themselves and others accountable for closing this performance gap. They model and teach the appropriate behaviors that strengthen both technical skills and motivation.

A critical problem in management generally (not just in health care) is the scarcity of leaders who possess the influential leadership behaviors that propel organizations to greatness and guide them through the significant challenges of today. We have plenty of managers and leaders who have superb technical, operational, and financial skills and an acute understanding of system processes. But we lack managers and leaders who have the motivation to go beyond those skills to enable the organization to exceed (not just meet) expectations; keep patients safe; and continue to improve processes, quality, and satisfaction. We lack leaders who have a deep understanding of the link between behavior and peak performance.

In the book *Good to Great*, author Jim Collins and his colleagues present evidence that behind a high-performing organization is an influential leader.[1] This finding emphasizes one simple truth: Influential leaders not only can close the performance gap but also can inspire others to make a difference. State-of-the-art equipment, technical and operational expertise, and use of proven quality improvement methodologies (e.g., benchmarking, Six Sigma, Lean Manufacturing) are merely tools that help leaders and cannot, on their own, bring about excellent performance. The key to excellence, as Collins and other researchers have found, remains the influential leader. A study of 10,000 followers published in *Gallup Management Journal* reveals that people are looking for trust, compassion, stability, and hope from their leaders.[2] Researcher Barry Conchie states: "[t]rust also speaks to behavioral predictability."[3]

Now is the time to invest in developing influential leaders.

Leadership Development

Recently I asked this question to a group of health care professionals attending my leadership seminar: Where do you learn how to *be* a leader? I clarified my question with "I am not asking for the typical traits of a good leader. I want to know your experiences in how to 'do' leadership."

The answers were strikingly similar. None of the leaders in attendance had received any formal training, although many of them had taken continuing education courses in leadership theories and nearly everyone had read a best-selling (and trendy) management book. None had been exposed to the influential leadership concept and its associated behaviors.

This finding is not surprising. Many health care leaders (at all organizational levels) today came into their titled positions by being exemplary employees or followers. These former "line people" were exceptional at their day-to-day responsibilities and were rewarded with a promotion, but they have had little or no training (formal or informal) or experience in leadership and management. Few organizations invest the time and money to develop or prepare their most capable employees for future leadership positions. Even more unfortunate is that many existing leadership development programs ignore the value of studying human behaviors and the impact of these behaviors on performance outcomes. Without proper training and experience in how to do their jobs, new leaders are clueless about how to deal with the dysfunctional situations and behaviors (or "people issues") that occur daily and could consume 80 percent of their workday.

Leadership development should revolve around issues that are most relevant to leaders, such as how to hire or retain talented people. Effective leadership development is hands on, not lecture oriented or discussion based. Learned concepts must be practiced, applied to actual situations, and repeated until mastered. Feedback on performance should also be sought.

Why Leadership Development Efforts Fail

A number of factors contribute to the failure of leadership development programs. Among these is the limited participation by senior leadership in the training and in holding people accountable for changing behavior following the training. Limited participation signals a lack of commitment. As one common saying explains, "The difference between participation and commitment is like an eggs-and-ham breakfast: The chicken participated, but the pig was committed."

Another reason that leadership development efforts fail is the cynicism of senior leaders. These leaders resist investing time and money into development programs, convinced that such efforts will yield minimal benefits but require maximum resources. This mind-set is disastrous, and it communicates to talented employees that the organization is not concerned about their growth. Remember that people do not quit their jobs; they quit their leaders.

When an organization fails to develop its leaders, or worse, when an organization develops leaders and loses them to another organization, the impact on organizational performance is staggering.

What This Book Offers

Thousands of books and articles on leadership have been published, and most of them contain specific definitions of and strategies for leadership. With all of these resources, leaders still lack the basic ability to apply what they know to what they do. This book's focus on behavior (rather than technical skills) and on doing (in addition to knowing) sets it apart from other leadership publications. Here, I present the C^4 model, a framework for assessing and understanding behavior.

A lot of material in this book is culled from the leadership seminars and workshops I lead. Attendees had expressed their wish for a compilation of the material distributed and discussed in those seminars, and my efforts to deliver on that wish presented an opportunity to write a book. The straightforward and conversational style of this book will resonate with people. Clear presentation of this information will clarify many leadership concepts and, I hope, will persuade you to try them for your benefit and the benefit of your organization and the community it serves.

Focus on Behavior, Not Technical Skills

Pick up the last five best-selling books on leadership, and you will find the same lists of attributes that are heavy on technical elements but light on behavior and relationship skills. It is the latter that bring out the technical competencies and enable the job to be done well. At higher levels of leadership (e.g., chief executives), technical skills are less important than good behavior and relationship-building ability. The reason is that the work of senior leaders is more strategic than operational.

Look at the number of highly capable leaders in politics, business, and nonprofit sectors who have failed. The root cause has not been their lack of talent, desire, ambition, enthusiasm, passion, agility, and other qualities. What sends these otherwise successful leaders hurtling toward the ground is their poor behavior. They become so insulated by their sense of self-worth and value that they lose sight of how they relate to others and get separated from those who can give them honest feedback.

Behavioral attributes (including interrelations ability), commonly and incorrectly referred to as "soft skills," are really the "hard skills" that enable the leader to be influential—self-aware, collaborative, and connective. Employees' low morale, refusal to engage in their work, mistrust of management, lack of motivation, and poor performance are linked to their leaders' consistent display of negative behavior. It is easier to overlook someone's technical shortcomings than his poor interpersonal skills. A leader's behavior is the most important predictor of organizational performance.

Shift in Leadership Thinking

Highly successful people are protective of the behavior they believe is the source of their success. This protectiveness is supported by confirmation bias. *Confirmation bias* is a type of selective thinking or a tendency to gravitate toward facts and data that support what an individual already believes to be true.

In my experience, many leaders do not see their negative behaviors as the root cause of the safety, quality, and service problems they encounter in the workplace. Their confirmation bias is strong, and they are often ready to show evidence from the literature that something else is the source of their performance challenges. One conclusion is absolutely true: Behavior lapses are obvious to everyone but the person who commits them.

This book is a call for a radical shift in leadership thinking—from one that focuses on technical elements and processes to one that considers the impact of poor behavior on safety, quality, and service. This change must start with leaders at all levels. Real change will never come from outside consultants or the latest management fad. It will come from within an organization whose leaders understand the power of being self-aware, collaborative, and connective and are willing to unleash that power.

People tend to change their behavior when they understand how it affects (negatively or positively) the outcome of their work, the lives of those around them, and the overall performance of their organization. For example, when a nurse supervisor explains to a verbally aggressive nurse that her behavior intimidates her co-workers and compromises her patient's health, she is more likely to change or tone down her approach. Another example is when the pharmacy director changes the "mental map" or "mental script" of weary pharmacists by asking them to think of their job as enhancing the patients' quality of life and not merely as filling hundreds of prescription orders every day. The former thought process trumps the latter because it supports the fact that pharmacists play an active role in patient care and as such should display behaviors that reflect the purpose of their position.

These simple techniques are used by influential leaders, who have a non-negotiable commitment to excellence and to their employees.

Organization of This Book

The book is organized into three parts, which correspond to the three fundamental principles of influential leadership.

Part I—Self-Awareness—explores the ancient Greek aphorism "know thyself." Virtually every kind of performance problem and personal or professional conflict is the result of relationship dysfunction. This dysfunction stems from a lack of self-awareness. Our own quirks and habits are invisible to us, so we do not see how they affect those around us. Part I (chapters 1 through 3) guides you to discover the mental patterns that drive thoughts and actions. Influential leaders are keenly aware of their own patterns, so they are able to effectively manage their emotions, conflicts, and relationships. They are empathic and compassionate, traits that come from knowing their own preferences and emotional needs. Part I helps you analyze how you deal with others and why, so that you can improve your thoughts and behaviors to become a leader who energizes, engages, and enhances the lives of those around you.

Part II—Collaboration—addresses the necessary elements of building a collaborative organizational culture. No one can achieve greatness alone. Success is the product of a highly functional team, and creating such a team requires strong interpersonal skills more than technical acumen. In part II (chapters 4 through 6), the roles of trust and accountability in building a collaborative culture are discussed.

Part III—Connection—elaborates on a simple but often overlooked concept: People perform activities better when they feel emotionally connected with what they are doing and with whom they are doing it. Before people buy into the organization's mission and vision, they must first buy into its leader. Part III (chapters 7 and 8) describes the factors that compel people to follow their leaders, the many ways that connections can be made and sustained, and the connection pitfalls that leaders must avoid.

Conclusion

This book is a collection of my life's work in health care leadership research, teaching, and coaching. A great many leaders are struggling to lead their organizations effectively. They have the desire but lack this basic understanding about behaviors:

1. They are the building blocks of organizational culture and performance.
2. They are vital to establishing and sustaining the organization's operational, financial, strategic, clinical, and human resources functions.

The concept of influential leadership is not a quick fix or a fad. It requires a commitment to achieving real breakthroughs. It requires learning; a change of mind-set; and a rediscovery of your work's passion, meaning, value, and purpose. Are you willing to try it?

Your ability to become an influential leader is directly proportional to your ability to manage your behavior and the way it affects others. Just a few bad habits can nullify your influence on people or leave a false impression that behavior has no impact on organizational, departmental, or team performance. An excerpt from my poem "Born into This World" may say my point best:

> Deming, Juran, now Toyota's our savior,
> When will we get it, the answer's behavior.

Albert Einstein wrote: "The significant problems we face cannot be solved at the same level of thinking we were at when we created them." The good news is that we can change, and this book offers the tools for doing so. Read on.

Key Takeaways

- This book calls for a radical shift in leadership thinking—from one that focuses on technical elements and processes to one that considers the impact of poor behavior on safety, quality, and service.
- Organizations that blossom and flourish are those whose leaders understand the fundamental principles of influential leadership (self-awareness, collaboration, and connection) and have the discipline to intentionally and purposefully apply the behaviors associated with these principles.
- A self-aware leader is in a better position to self-manage than one who lacks this awareness. Such a leader, then, is better able to collaborate and connect with others.
- Influential leaders rely on the principle of collaboration: People, not processes, strengthen or weaken the organization's pursuit of performance excellence.
- When people are emotionally disconnected from their leaders, they are emotionally disconnected from their work and its accomplishment.
- State-of-the-art equipment, technical and operational expertise, and use of proven quality improvement meth-

odologies are merely tools. They cannot, on their own, bring about excellent performance.

- Employees' low morale, refusal to engage in their work, mistrust of management, lack of motivation, and poor performance are linked to their leaders' consistent display of negative behavior.
- People tend to change their behavior when they understand how it affects (negatively or positively) the outcome of their work, the lives of those around them, and the overall performance of their organization.

Applying the Concepts of Influential Leadership

The following questions are intended to initiate self-examination of your journey to become an influential leader.

1. Would you follow *yourself* as a leader?
    - What is your strongest leadership attribute?
    - How does this attribute influence those around you?
    - If you were to ask others to identify your top three leadership strengths, what would they say?
    - Do you allow other people an opportunity to expose your behavioral weaknesses (through seeking feedback)?
    - Do you see yourself as an influential leader? Why and how?

2. Who are the influential leaders in your life?
    - What behavioral traits does each display? What traits do they have in common?
    - What do you admire most about them?
    - How did they influence you to be the person you are today?
    - Why would you emulate their behaviors?

3. Are you constantly engaged in your self-development?
   - Do you have a personal mission statement?
   - Can you list your top three values without stopping to think about them?
   - Do you commit a regular part of your schedule to learning something new about leadership?
   - Are your behaviors aligned with your non-negotiable moral principles or values?

4. In your current position, who do you recognize as an influential leader?
   - When this leader offers advice, why do other people listen?
   - Do you want to be around this leader to learn from his or her behaviors, actions, abilities, and effectiveness?
   - Do you find this leader to be realistic in acknowledging the challenges of the organization yet highly optimistic and accepting of the responsibility to find solutions for these obstacles?

References

1. J. Collins, *Good to Great: Why Some Companies Make the Leap . . . and Others Don't* (New York: HarperBusiness, 2001).
2. *Gallup Management Journal*, "What Followers Want from Leaders," 2009 [http://gmj.gallup.com/content/113542/What-Followers-Want-From-Leaders.aspx]. Accessed August 11, 2010.
3. T. Rath and B. Conchie, *Strengths-Based Leadership: Great Leaders, Teams, and Why People Follow* (Washington, DC: Gallup Press, 2009).

PART

I

What Is Self-Awareness?

Nothing so conclusively proves a man's ability to lead others as what he does from day to day to lead himself.
—Thomas J. Watson, former president of IBM

Self-awareness is the first principle of influential leadership. It is the basic competency of influential leaders and is the first step toward improving professional and personal areas in life. Self-awareness is essential to changing behavior that hinders performance excellence. You cannot replace old beliefs, thoughts, and habits without understanding what and why you need to change. As mentioned in the Introduction, your behavior deficiencies are obvious to everyone but you.

Self-awareness has three components: (1) volitional, which is addressed in chapter 2; (2) mental, addressed in chapter 2; and (3) emotional, addressed in chapter 3. These components correspond with the first three dimensions of a behavior assessment framework I call the *C⁴ model*. The C⁴ dimensions are (1) conviction, (2) convincing, (3) compelling, and (4) conforming (which aligns with collaboration and connection, the other two principles of influential leadership). The C⁴ model is described fully in chapter 1 and is applied to the topics in subsequent chapters.

Influential leaders are self-aware. They have the discipline and intention to look inward on a regular basis to assess their thoughts, beliefs, and behavior so that they do not act impulsively, they continue to be fair, and they behave according to their internal compass. This focus on self-awareness drives daily behaviors that encourage collaboration and connection. Failure to take the steps to self-awareness leads to dysfunctional relationships, multiple conflicts, and poor performance. These consequences are evident in both personal and professional pursuits.

Self-awareness leads to self-management, and self-management leads to self-mastery. You cannot change what you do not know exists, and you cannot improve on what you do not know is a problem.

1

Self-Awareness: The Basic Competency of the Influential Leader

The truth is that you cannot improve what you cannot manage, and you cannot manage what you are blind to in your personal habits and behavior.

—Tim Kight, organizational development expert

Self-awareness is an honest understanding of your own values, desires, thought patterns, motivations, goals and ambitions, emotional responses, strengths and weaknesses, and effect on others. This awareness takes years to fully develop, requires commitment, and is supplemented by others' feedback. Once developed and practiced regularly, self-awareness enables you to manage your behavior, improve your interactions and relationships, and gain or increase your influence.

The level of self-awareness is related to the level of influence and performance: The more self-aware a leader is, the more influential she is and the better her followers perform. As Daniel Goleman, a thought leader in the area of emotional intelligence, explains in his book *Primal Leadership*, "Leaders high in emotional self-awareness are attuned to their inner signals, recognizing how their feelings affect them and their job performance. Leaders with high self-awareness typically know their strengths and limitations and exhibit a gracefulness in learning where they need to improve."[1]

Research in business, behavioral science, and organizational development states that influential leaders and peak-performing organizations have a highly developed sense of themselves and their identities.[2] They understand their behavior preferences, manage their emotions, and are keenly aware of the need to create and sustain interpersonal relationships. Influential leaders are empathic (i.e., they can relate to others' emotions and experiences) and compassionate (i.e., they are genuinely concerned for the plight of others). Conversely, the lack of self-awareness is a primary cause of ineffective leadership, which poisons the organizational culture. Sadly, most organizations avoid fixing the biggest internal constraint on their success—leaders who are not held accountable for their less-than-desirable interpersonal skills. Mission, vision, and values statements that adorn the hallways of the organization are not meaningful if the daily behaviors of its leaders contradict the moral and spiritual essence that the organization claims to espouse. Self-examination reveals the behaviors that act as barriers and derail performance.

One reason many leaders are reluctant to become self-aware is that they are unsure of what it means to be a leader. As mentioned in the Introduction, many managers do not receive training on how to "do" leadership. As a result, they do not understand that leadership entails far more than budgeting or scheduling, for example; it also involves negotiating with people and preventing dysfunctions. Leadership means inspiring and mobilizing people to accomplish something of lasting value, something that makes a difference in people's lives. This responsibility for other people must be made clear so that leaders can be convinced of their need to become self-aware. Without self-awareness, leaders will not see that their behavior affects how their employees engage with their work, behave toward each other, and treat their patients.

Another reason for this reluctance about self-awareness is that it holds leaders to their own core values, which then makes it difficult for leaders to adjust to a popular or common belief or practice with which they do not agree. Finding harmony between the self and the outside world is ideal, and conflict is likely to ensue if the values of the self are not aligned with those of the organization. You can only pretend to be something you are not for a limited time. Ultimately, under a certain circumstance (e.g., fatigue, stress), your real character and beliefs will manifest through your behavior. Regardless of the outcome (negative or positive) of the journey to self-awareness, it is a worthwhile road to take for all leaders.

This chapter explains the various elements of self-awareness, including its most critical component—change. Change not only is inevitable in health care but also is a requirement in an individual becoming an influential leader, so it is discussed extensively in this chapter. The C^4 model, a framework I created, is introduced here to guide readers in understanding and assessing their behavior.

Self-Examination

Self-examination is the fastest route to self-awareness. Yet, a great many leaders do not take a look inside, possibly afraid of what they might find. The irony is that these same leaders are masters at conducting root-cause analyses on the failures of their organization. However, such examinations often do not lead to improvement or change in processes. Still other leaders choose to cope with organizational problems rather than evaluate and then solve them. That is the easy, but dead-end, road to take.

What is true of organizations is also true of individuals. Leaders are not perfect beings, much like organizations are not perfect entities. That truth is reason enough to signal a need for self-examination. Add to this fact the interpersonal conflicts or behavioral clashes that leaders face on a daily basis, and you have all the indicators that something is wrong somewhere and it must be addressed. Do not mistake behavioral conflicts for personality or style issues, because they are different. Behavior is a matter of choice, while personality is an inherent trait. Self-examination is the key to making the right behavior choice and to recognizing poor habits.

Sincerity

Self-examination reveals many things, including our level of sincerity, which is a trait all influential leaders share. Sincerity is synonymous with genuineness, honesty, and authenticity. Gather a group of people, then ask each of them to list the attributes of the "ideal" leader. Sincerity will appear on each list. I know because I have conducted this exercise with various individuals from different organizations.

Merriam-Webster's Dictionary notes that *sincere* is from Middle French meaning "honest," which in turn is derived from the Latin *sincerus*, meaning "whole, unsullied, pure, honest, and genuine." A story of unknown origin states that the literal meaning of *sincerus* is "without wax." During the Middle Ages, defective marble artwork was commonly repaired by grounding marble chips into dust, mixing the dust with wax, and applying the mixture to the defect, which was thus disguised. Marble artwork without defects was called *sincerus* or "without wax."

It is a great story, even if it may be untrue.

The point here is simple: Leaders must all be without wax. Crises, stress, and other difficulties reveal people's inner character and pretenses. Sooner or later, under the heat of a trying circumstance, the real you will become evident. So ask yourself a reflective question: How whole, unsullied, pure, honest, and genuine am I as a leader, and do I behave accordingly?

Feedback

Do you know what behaviors you display on a daily basis? Are your habits bringing you closer to or preventing you from achieving the high levels of performance necessary to make a significant difference in people's lives? These questions can be answered by self-examination, using a feedback system.

The very thought of feedback generates an immediate emotional reaction. The reason is twofold:

1. We do not want (or are afraid) to hear how people experience us through our behavior.

2. Other people do not want to give us feedback for fear of retaliation or ruining our relationship.

This emotional dynamic applies to both personal and professional situations. For example, a wife is afraid to tell her husband to control his road rage because she is physically threatened by him, while her husband does not want to hear criticisms about his driving. Likewise, a staff member does not want to tell his boss that her unwillingness to solicit ideas and suggestions from the team is stifling creativity, while the boss avoids communication with her staff for fear of their judgment. Regardless of the awkwardness inherent in giving and taking feedback, all leaders (and staff) need to engage in it to demonstrate their commitment to self-examination and self-improvement.

Influential leaders solicit regular feedback from their colleagues and followers. They are committed to all kinds of improvement and understand that how they think and behave affects the way they lead. Influential leaders fully support the organizational mission and vision, and they ensure that their personal values and purpose align with those of the organization. They serve selflessly, unconcerned about preserving their egos or protecting their authority. They believe in and display transparency in everything they do, and getting feedback is one means of ensuring that this transparency continues and that self-improvement never ends. As German philosopher Johann Goethe said, "self-knowledge is best learned, not by contemplation but by action."

If you want to be an influential leader, you must seek out and welcome honest and consistent feedback on your behavior. Assure those whom you asked for feedback that they are safe from retaliation and animosity, and encourage them to be as candid as possible. Your response to people who provide you with feedback will demonstrate your level of sincerity and ensure their continued willingness to provide feedback in the future.

Executive coach and author Marshall Goldsmith describes people's usual reaction to positive and negative feedback. He says that we all tend to accept feedback that is compatible to what we believe to be true and reject feedback that does not match our sense of reality.[3] This concept is akin to pattern recognition—that is, our brains gravitate toward information that is known, familiar, or concrete. For example, if a nurse executive receives feedback that she is a poor listener, she may become defensive and deem the comment an insult. After all, she may argue, she did not rise to her current position by not paying attention to others' needs and wants along the way. Thus, she will ignore the feedback altogether, rendering the process a waste of time and effort. This example could apply to all levels of employees in all kinds of jobs.

The way feedback is delivered determines whether the feedback process will be ineffective or constructive. Constructive feedback yields productive outcomes because its intention is to coach and inform, rather than to blame and accuse. Even negative feedback can be turned into actionable goals when the feedback is delivered in a constructive manner. According to Goldsmith, constructive feedback requires the following steps:

1. Ask the right people.
2. Ask the right questions.
3. Interpret the answers properly.
4. Accept the responses as accurate.

Results obtained from constructive feedback may then be fitted into the Johari window and its variant, the Nohari window. Created in 1955 by Joe Luft and Harry Ingham, the Johari and Nohari windows are practical tools for self-examination of one's interactions and relationships with others. You can find illustrations of both tools and instructions for how to employ them on several Web sites such as the following:

http://kevan.org/johari
www.businessballs.com/johariwindowmodel.htm
www.mindtools.com/CommSkll/JohariWindow.htm

Many feedback tools are available, with varying degrees of effectiveness and practicality. Regardless of the system you use, do not lose sight of its essence: Change begins with seeking feedback and diligently applying the lessons learned. As a result, we can move from complacency, fear, and doubt to improved behavior, creative thought processes, mental toughness, and discipline—all of which help us to shape or re-create our lives and to make optimal life choices.

Four Approaches to Becoming an Influential Leader

John Maxwell, an internationally known and respected leadership expert, has said "Leading me has always been my greatest challenge as a leader. . . . Acknowledging that leading myself is a challenge brings back some painful memories." Maxwell suggests these four approaches to becoming an influential leader:[4]

1. *Learn to follow before you try to lead.* If you submit yourself to the leadership of another, you will become more humble. This experience teaches you to appreciate the hard work, sacrifices, and frustrations of being a follower. In this capacity, you will learn to listen, to wait your turn, and to be open to alternatives you would not consider in normal circumstances.
2. *Develop self-discipline.* Self-discipline is an exercise in mental and emotional strength. It is not easy to practice in an ever-changing, chaotic environment, and developing it does not happen overnight. Once mastered, however, self-discipline is a powerful ally against all kinds of personal and professional challenges.
3. *Practice patience.* Overworking or working too fast rarely produces consistent, strategic, and sustainable performance. Instead, it burns you out and gets you too far ahead of your followers and not alongside them. Your pace should be aligned with that of your followers so that you can stay connected. Learn and teach along the way.

4. *Seek accountability.* Leadership is seductive and delusional. It allows people to indulge their ego and forget their convictions. You should demand transparency from yourself and others. You should also remind yourself regularly that you are accountable to everyone around you.

Initiating Change in Ourselves and Others

Becoming self-aware means discovering what works, what does not work, and what could use a little or a lot of work. In this process, change is almost always required. Change is neither easy nor popular, whether we want to make it happen for ourselves or inspire others to make a change. It is difficult for two reasons.

First, neuroscience has discovered that physically our brain does not want to cooperate with our decision to change.[5] Once the brain learns consistent patterns of behavior, even dysfunctional ones, it hangs on to those patterns, which are phenomenally strong. The good news is that we can retrain our brain, albeit with a good deal of consistent, hard effort. Second, change is a personal and intimate endeavor. We can order someone else to make a change and, perhaps, even give that person an ultimatum or a list of dire consequences. We can offer full support and encouragement, motivate the effort, teach practical strategies, and regularly follow up on the progress. But we cannot make the person commit to that change if he is not able, willing, and/or ready. Simply, people must have their own desire to change. Without this desire, our behavioral modification and change initiatives will fail.

Let's illustrate this concept with the actual problem that health care organizations face when they implement best-practice approaches to improving safety, quality, and service in hopes of replicating the outcomes and rewards these approaches have brought to other hospitals. The intention behind this effort is noble—one that nearly everyone can agree on. After all, best practice is known to result in higher productivity, effectiveness, efficiency, and satisfaction in all operational and clinical areas. The dilemma starts in the organizational expectation that if the best-practice model is followed exactly or at least closely, then it will yield the same outcomes; that is, if the approach reduced Hospital A's medical error rate, then it should reduce Hospital B's medical error rate as well. This expectation is logical, but it does not take into account the variations between the two hospitals.

One such variation involves people—from chief executives to administrators to clinicians to support staff. People of two organizations are not the same, and neither are their thought patterns, attitudes, and behaviors toward the change process. Although "push back" to any change can be expected in all organizations, it is especially toxic in some cultures. Consequently, this resistance and people's thought and behavioral patterns, as well as their desire to change, alter the outcomes of a best-practice initiative from one organization to the next.

What we know to be true of many high-performing organizations and individuals is that they rarely benchmark or measure themselves against the results of their competitors. They opt to compete against themselves, adjusting their processes, strategies, behaviors, and mind-set to suit their own purpose, objectives, and expectations. They control their performance and outcomes, not the other way around. Marginal performers, on the other hand, follow the herd mentality, choosing tactics and plans developed by others and hoping the results are generalizable to all.

The Three Deadly "Ds" of Change

Resistance to change has three stages: denial, defending, and diminishing. When applied to changing behavior, the stages work as follows:

1. *Denial* is a person's natural tendency to dismiss behavior that is disruptive, dysfunctional, or unproductive. To

admit to such a behavior is self-incriminating, so in an effort to avoid others' judgment, the person resorts to denial.

2. *Defending* is a way to stand up for or justify the existence of the behavior, and it comes after a person is no longer able to refute that the habit is evident. The person is prepared to name the self-perceived benefits or advantages of the behavior and to counter any and all opposing views.

3. *Diminishing* is the stage at which the person turns against those who urge him to change the behavior. This response is a deliberate attempt to deflect focus away from the change, especially when the need becomes undeniable, and to "shoot the messenger." The person will question and minimize the credibility and character of the other people involved to make the case that his behavior is just fine and the fault lies with others.

At any of these stages, the person's level of performance is lowered and his judgment is compromised. When these outcomes occur in a health care setting, everything and everyone suffer, including patients. Now imagine that the person who resists change is an authority figure—someone in charge of operations, finances, strategic and tactical plans, clinical care, quality, or community relations. How would this leader guide the organizational efforts if he routinely relied on the three deadly Ds of change? As mentioned in the Introduction, an individual leader's behavior is the most important predictor of organizational performance. A leader who is unwilling to improve and help himself is unwilling to improve and help his organization.

The Motivation to Change

The collective, general mission statement of health care organizations—to provide care and comfort to the sick—should be a sufficient motivator for change. Influential leaders understand, however, that this mission alone is not enough. In fact, even intolerable outcomes are sometimes insufficient to ignite and propel real behavior change. What is needed is to tap into people's desire to change—to do something else and to believe they are capable of doing so and achieving results. Chapter 2 further discusses motivations to change, including dissatisfaction and a sense of urgency.

Influential leaders are keenly aware of the need to create an organizational culture in which people are encouraged to take personal responsibility for doing their jobs well and to be accountable for their own actions. In this type of culture, people discover the most effective and efficient solutions on their own and realize that those solutions already reside within the organization; they are not brought in by external "change experts" or copied from "top" organizations. Simply, a culture that trusts and respects its people's knowledge and abilities as well as inspires, teaches, and expects them to perform at high levels increases the motivation to change and improve.

A word of warning is due at this juncture. Not everyone in an organization has the desire to perform at high levels or to change the status quo, and some people deliberately sabotage change initiatives to avoid doing more work or learning new things. Influential leaders are realistic about these types of followers, opting to let them go instead of waiting for their toxic behaviors to affect the whole enterprise. (See part II for more discussion on this issue.)

The C⁴ Model: A Behavioral Assessment Tool

Self-awareness requires intentional behavior change. To initiate this change, a methodology that incorporates different theories of behavior should be used; this approach ensures that behavior-related factors are examined in a comprehensive manner. The C^4 model is ideal for this purpose.

The C^4 model is an integrated framework for understanding and assessing behavior. It questions existing habits; focuses on areas that need change; and emphasizes the importance of accepting personal responsibility, taking initiative, managing emotions, and committing to continuous learning and development. It poses self-examination questions such as the following:

1. What do I believe is true about me and the world around me?
2. What do I think about my relationships with others?
3. How do I manage my emotional energy, and what script or narrative have I created for myself and for others?
4. How do I choose my relationships, and are these relationships aligned with my thoughts, beliefs, and attitudes?

The C^4 model can be used for both personal behavior change and organizational change efforts.

The C^4 Components

C^4 stands for the four components—conviction, convincing, compelling, and conforming—that must be examined in order for behavior change to occur. Each element can be linked to the three principles of influential leadership—self-awareness, collaboration, and connection. The first three—conviction, convincing, and compelling—are associated with self-awareness (discussed in part I of this book), and the fourth—conforming—is related to collaboration and connection (discussed in parts II and III). For an illustration of the C^4 model, see figure 1-1. Following is an explanation of each component.

Conviction is the "why" of behavior. Conviction is a strongly held belief that guides actions. By examining our convictions, we can begin to understand how our values inform our daily behavior and identify gaps between the two. In other words, conviction asks "Why am I doing what I am doing?"

Convincing is the "what" of behavior. This component revolves around our mental models—the perceptions, biases, notions, and other cognitive patterns that enable us to understand and deal with the external world. These mental models develop over time, and they either help or hinder change. Convincing requires candid examination of how our thoughts influence our decisions, behaviors, interactions, and performance. The goal is to replace dysfunctional thinking or reframe our mind-set so that we are more open to positive experiences, such as learning, developing creative or innovative solutions, and seeking mutually beneficial relationships and pursuits. In other words, convincing asks "What am I thinking when I do the things I do?"

Figure 1-1.   Influential Leadership and the Components of the C⁴ Model

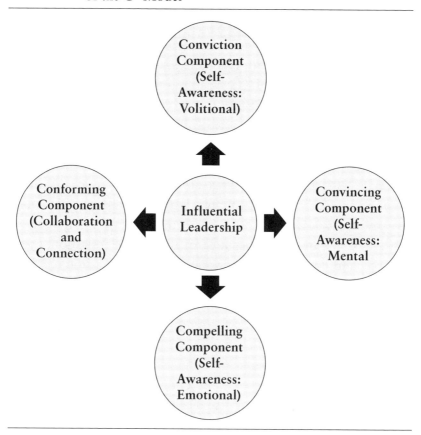

Compelling is the "how" of behavior. This component assesses our level of emotional control. Our ability to positively engage others and respond to their needs is a direct result of our ability to manage our emotions. This display of interest and care in others serves as a compelling reason for change; conversely, it compels people to resist change. People almost always buy into a leader before they buy into his vision. No proven process, tool, or performance improvement program can trump an effective leader's connection with people, because change is an emotional act, and the more emotionally engaged the followers are to their leader, the more compelled they are to support him and to mimic his emotional control. In other words, compelling asks "How do I express my emotions, and how do my emotions affect my performance and others' perception of me and my abilities?"

Conforming is the "who" of behavior. This component relates to the "others"—our team members and collaboration partners, from senior management to staff to physicians. In a collaboration or any team setting, most failures are caused by poor communication, lack of cooperation, and fragmentation of teams. These are all behavioral weaknesses that many leaders do not recognize. Conforming entails learning, teaching, and modeling ideal practices with the purpose of transforming individualist thinking and behavior that are not conducive to the needs of a collaborative culture. In other words, conforming asks "Who on my team display behaviors that either help or hinder collaboration, cooperation, and connection, and what can I do to encourage good behaviors and correct the poor ones?"

The point of the C^4 model is simple: Personal and organizational change requires an understanding of why we behave a certain way (conviction); what mental patterns we follow to justify our behavior (convincing); how our emotions affect our performance and influence others' perception and support (compelling); and who on our team displays behavior that impedes team functioning, and what must be done to correct it (conforming).

Finding Your Behavior Strengths

Change and chaos are constant in our knowledge- and technology-driven world. Yet, with all this change and chaos, both influential leaders and their organizations continue to thrive. What distinguishes influential leaders from those who fail? Research has found a common denominator among successful leaders: They play to their behavior strengths. Following is a great illustration of this principle.

Patrick Charmel, president and chief executive officer of Griffin Hospital in Derby, Connecticut, plays to his strengths and embodies the principles of influential leadership. Charmel places tremendous emphasis on his strength of building relationships with people. In fact, he is known to spend more time in various departments than in his office.[6] As a result, employee satisfaction at Griffin is high, which in turn drives up its safety, quality, and service results. Griffin has been consistently named in *Fortune* magazine's "100 Best Companies to Work For" list, has earned Planetree's designation as a patient-centered hospital, and has received several honors for its clinical care and leadership excellence.[7] Griffin's culture is marked by open communication, trust, and integrity.[8]

Influential leaders like Patrick Charmel know that by placing emphasis on building their strengths they can mitigate the impact of their weaknesses.[9] Rather than try to compensate for their own level of performance in an area of weakness, influential leaders build highly functional teams and surround themselves with the right people to compensate for their own performance inadequacies. Influential leaders are so secure in who they are and what they believe that they aggressively seek out team members who balance their strengths and weaknesses.

One misconception about the playing-to-your-strength strategy is that it prevents a person from trying a new approach or imposes a limitation in the event of an organizational or market change. Another fear is that the successes gained from this strategy are short term and may derail a person's career because all he knows to do is to stick to what he does well. These beliefs may be true from the technical skills perspective, and I do recommend that leaders continue to learn and expand their technical skills. But behaviorally, this kind of thinking is uninformed. Behavior drives technical skill, and if a leader leverages his behavior strength and leans on other behavior domains to support him, he can bring about improved technical performance, better interrelationships, innovative solutions to problems, and consistent positive outcomes.

Domains of Leadership Strength

The strategy of playing to your strengths starts with discovering what your strong points are. Tom Rath and Barry Conchie classify leadership strengths into four domains: (1) executing (driver), (2) influencing (persuader), (3) strategic thinking (analyzer), and (4) relationship building (stabilizer). According to this model, each of us has a behavior preference represented by one of these four domains, but we also have the capacity to flex toward the other three domains.[10] Peak performance is the optimal blending of all the behavior dynamics within these domains. Your behavior preference (or strength domain) determines how you see the world around you, but it represents only 25 percent of your capacity for problem solving and creative thinking. If you are a "driver" who demands that everyone in the organization think and behave as a driver, you lower the level of organizational performance by excluding the strengths of the other three domains.

Your strength domain increases your potential for success. It shapes the way you function in the critical areas of performance, such as communicating, visioning, processing information, thinking creatively, managing emotions, aligning your core values, and relating to other people. Thus, awareness of the dominant strength as well as other domains is essential under times of stress, change, fatigue, and chaos because it enables us to be grounded on who we are, what we believe in, and how to behave accordingly.

Influential leaders know their behavior strengths and allow them to dominate when they are seeking the most optimal outcomes in relationships and performance. Furthermore, influential leaders understand the power of collaboration and connection (the other two principles of influential leadership), so they create a team composed of people who have strengths in all four domains. In this blend and balance of strengths, influential leaders propel their organizations to a higher level of performance.

Behavior Preference Tools

A number of behavior preference tools are available in the marketplace. These tools can be used to identify your strength domain and may be coupled with a feedback mechanism. I highly encourage you to seek out and use these tools.

Suppose a behavior preference tool identified you as a dominant "analyzer" who is good at strategic thinking. People will experience your behavior as cautious, careful, consistent, and diplomatic. You can have a profound effect on your team with your constant pursuit of getting the details right. But your endless quest for data can cause "analysis paralysis" for your team. The analyzer in this example lacks self-awareness and is oblivious to her behavior's impact on others. By seeking and receiving feedback, this analyzer can learn to gravitate toward domains that are more accommodating and, in the process, enhance the team's performance. During this behavior change, other members of the team can become more receptive to and welcoming of the analyzer's dominant behavior strength.

A person who is at his best in performance, productivity, safety, quality, and service, playing to his strength as an analyzer, needs to function with behaviors that are suited to that domain. Alternatively, a person who is a "persuader," playing to her strength as being influential, can flex to the domains of the analyzer, the stabilizer, and the driver. This person can accommodate the compatible strength domains of other team members without having to become like them. Influential leaders embrace the diversity of these domains and create the vision and cultures to leverage the strengths of each person to propel them to higher levels of organizational performance.

Conclusion

Self-awareness is essential to changing behaviors that hinder performance excellence. Its three dimensions are (1) volitional, (2) mental, and (3) emotional, and these elements are discussed in subsequent chapters. Self-examination, feedback, and behavioral preference tools can help people assess their habits or tendencies. The C^4 model is a framework for understanding and making sustainable change. Successes in personal behavior change and organizational change are achieved because people want to change, and this desire is explained by various reasons. Sometimes, the reason may be that they realize the change is simply a better way to operate.

Life is the culmination of the choices we make, and one of these choices is how we behave. When we change what we think, we also change what we believe. When we change what we believe, we choose to change our habits and behaviors. Surprisingly, research has also shown the converse to be true. Sometimes, when faced with a significant challenge or severe problem, we choose to behave differently from our fundamental beliefs because doing so is the only effective course of action available.[11] We might say to ourselves "I may not understand why a new behavior produces more effective results, but I know that if I do it, I get better outcomes." Thus we begin to change our mind. Regardless of how we arrive at our decisions, when we effectively change how we behave, we transform ourselves, our organizations, and the communities we serve.

Key Takeaways

- Self-awareness is an honest understanding of your own values, desires, thought patterns, motivations, goals and ambitions, emotional responses, strengths and weaknesses, and effect on others.

- The level of self-awareness is related to the level of influence and performance: The more self-aware a leader is, the more influential she is and the better her followers perform.

- The lack of self-awareness is a primary cause of ineffective leadership, which poisons the organizational culture.

- Behavior is a matter of choice, while personality is an inherent trait. Self-examination is the key to making the right behavior choices and to recognizing poor habits.

- Constructive feedback yields productive outcomes because its intention is to coach and inform, rather than to blame and accuse.

- Resistance to change has three stages: (1) denial, (2) defending, and (3) diminishing.

- The C^4 model is a proactive tool for initiating change, questioning existing habits, maintaining focus, accepting personal responsibility, taking initiative, managing emotions, and committing to continuous learning.

- C^4 stands for the four components—conviction, convincing, compelling, and conforming—that must be examined and understood before change can occur.

- What distinguishes influential leaders from those who fail is that successful leaders play to their behavior strengths.

Applying the C^4 Model: Self-Awareness and the First Three Cs

The following questions are intended to initiate self-examination of your current way of thinking, behaving, working, leading, and interacting with others. Take the time to think about these questions, and be honest with yourself.

- Describe your understanding of self-awareness. Do you believe you are self-aware? If so, how do you maintain this awareness?

- Do you actively seek feedback on your behavior and performance? How often, and is the process structured or informal? Who is involved in providing this feedback? Are those people encouraged to be as honest as possible? What do you do with the information you receive? If you do not seek feedback, why not? How do you obtain comments, criticism, or suggestions otherwise?

- List your behavior traits (e.g., talkative) that you perceive cause or may cause interpersonal conflicts between you and your followers, colleagues, and friends. Alternatively, list repetitive habits that have been problematic in the past. How have you dealt with or corrected these traits? What barriers, if any, did you encounter in correcting them? Are you in denial of or defensive about these traits? Why? If not, are you committed to making a change?

- List your thinking patterns (e.g., overconfidence) that you perceive cause or may cause interpersonal problems between you and your followers, colleagues, and friends. Alternatively, list mental models that have been problematic in the past. How have you dealt with or corrected these thought patterns? What barriers, if any, did you encounter in correcting them? Are you in denial of or defensive about these patterns? Why? If not, are you committed to making a change?

- What do you allow your mind to dwell on? What thoughts come to your mind in moments of crisis or stress? Are these thoughts negative or positive?

- How do your thoughts affect your behavior and performance? In what specific ways can you change your thinking to change your behavior and influence your professional performance? The quality of your personal life? How motivated are you to change for the better to benefit yourself, your family, the staff, the organization, and the community? If you lack motivation, what do you need to stimulate your interest?

- Have you considered that the biggest fault you consistently see in others may be a reflection of your own glaring fault?
- When others share their experiences with you, how do you respond?
- How easily do you forgive yourself when you make a mistake that affects the lives of others? Have you considered that the degree to which you fail to forgive yourself is also the degree to which you fail to forgive others?

Complete this sentence: If I could do one thing differently to improve my relationship with *(fill in the blank),* I would *(describe the new behavior).*

References

1. D. Goleman, *Primal Leadership: Learning to Lead with Emotional Intelligence* (Boston: Harvard Business School Press, 2004, 253).
2. L. Ackerman, "The Identity Effect—Learning from the Inside Out," *Chief Learning Officer*, February 2010 [http://www.theidentitycircle.com/images/uploads/The_Identity_Effect_Learning_from_the_Inside_Out.pdf]. Accessed June 25, 2010.
3. M. Goldsmith, *What Got You Here Won't Get You There* (New York: Hyperion, 2007).
4. J.C. Maxwell, *Leadership Gold* (Nashville, TN: Thomas Nelson, 2008, 11–13).
5. R. Cooper, *Get Out of Your Own Way: The Five Keys to Surpassing Everyone's Expectations* (New York: Crown Business, 2006, 5).
6. K. Dempsey, "Personal Management: Play to Their Strengths," *Personnel Today*, 2007 [http://www.personneltoday.com/articles/2007/08/06/41795/performance-management-play-to-their-strengths.html]. Accessed June 25, 2010.

7. Griffin Hospital, "Performance Indicators: Awards and Recognition," 2010 [http://www.griffinhealth.org/AboutUs/Quality/Awards Recognition.aspx]. Accessed August 11, 2010.
8. Dempsey, "Personal Management."
9. P. Charmel, "CEO Best Practices Interview," *Human Capital Magazine* (March/April 2006): 12.
10. T. Rath and B. Conchie, *Strengths-Based Leadership: Great Leaders, Teams, and Why People Follow* (New York: Gallup Press, 2008, 23).
11. J. Sternin, "The Positive Deviance Initiative Story," *Policy Innovations*, 2007 [http://www.policyinnovations.org/ideas/innovations/data/PositiveDeviance]. Accessed June 25, 2010.

2

The Volitional and Mental Dimensions

You live with your thoughts,
so be careful what they are.
—Eva Arrington, author

Our heart is the seat of our deepest beliefs, or *convictions.* They are formed in our thoughts and guide our emotions, choices, biases, responses, and behaviors. They affect every aspect of our lives, including our work and performance. One example of how conviction drives performance is illustrated in the story of Ignaz Semmelweis (see figure 2-1). Both Semmelweis and his critics were promoting and behaving according to their respective beliefs, albeit at a high price, which is often the case in health care.

A caveat is in order: Basing your behavior on your convictions alone does not guarantee a quick, favorable outcome, as the Semmelweis story demonstrates. Conviction must be supported by volition—the conscious, willful act of making a decision. Volition, the first element of self-awareness, explains that what we choose to believe determines how we choose to behave, and vice versa. What we believe, in turn, is a product of our mental patterns—the culmination of our past and present experiences, observations, choices, practices, and circumstances. Being aware of these mental models enables us to manage our choices, including our behavior.

In this chapter, we explore these interrelated dimensions of self-awareness—volitional and mental—and their corresponding C^4 model elements—conviction and convincing.

Figure 2-1. Living by Conviction: An Example

Ignaz Semmelweis is a name few people recognize, but he was a man whose conviction was so strong that he stood by his beliefs and, in the process, made a lasting change in the lives of many people. In 1847, Professor Semmelweis was working at the Vienna General Hospital in Germany. At the time, many women who had recently given birth and their newborns were dying from puerperal fever (commonly called childbed fever), a form of septicemia. Most of these deaths occurred in physicians' clinics, not in the care of midwives. The common belief was that pregnant women and their babies had a greater chance of survival if the deliveries were performed by midwives rather than by physicians, and many women allegedly begged to be helped by midwives.

Semmelweis collected data, studied the clinics, and observed the situation. His finding confirmed that higher death rates were occurring at physicians' clinics than in midwives' practices. He was obsessed with the desire to discover the reason for this discrepancy. His initial hypothesis was that midwives only delivered babies whereas physicians did more, including performing autopsies and handling the sick. He knew that the answer lay in the differences in practices between midwives and physicians. He sacrificed the remainder of his life to finding the cause of and solution to this crisis.

He believed and demonstrated by practice that physicians could reduce the death rate by washing their hands with a chlorine solution before and after seeing a patient. Unfortunately, his hypothesis and recommendation ran counter to the prevailing medical knowledge of his day and met with powerful resistance. At the time, the medical establishment in Europe supported several popular theories about the origin of puerperal fever, such as it being caused by the weather or by "uncleanliness in the bowel," as a noted Hungarian physician claimed. The challenge to Semmelweis's assertions did not stop there. Many physicians were offended by the idea that they should be required to wash their hands. Despite the scientific justifications for the practice, physicians could not conceive of the notion that their gentlemen's hands could possibly be dirty. The convictions and status quo of the day were not going to change easily.

Semmelweis, who did not like to write or publish, was not interested in answering the criticism of his detractors. He did, however, convince medical students to try his recommendation. Sadly, he failed with the rest of the medical community, which was more concerned with its image than doing the right thing. One of Semmelweis's detractors was a physician who delivered his own niece's baby, refusing to abide by the recommended hand-washing protocol. The niece and the baby both died from puerperal fever. Overcome by guilt, the physician killed himself.

Figure 2-1. (Continued)

Later, Semmelweis was committed involuntarily to an insane asylum, where he contracted puerperal fever and died within two weeks. Some sources suggest that he was beaten to death by sanitarium staff, who might have been trying to stop his erratic attacks on physicians who remained resistant to his ideas. Eventually, chemist and bacteriologist Louis Pasteur was able to substantiate his microbial theory, vindicating the life's work of Ignaz Semmelweis.

Source: Adapted from "Ignaz Philipp Semmelweis (1818–65)" [about the cover], *Emerging Infectious Diseases* 7, no. 2 (2001) [http://www.cdc.gov/ncidod/EID/vol7no2/cover.htm]. Accessed June 25, 2010.

From Conviction to Volition

Today, hand washing has become the number one means of preventing the spread of disease. The Centers for Disease Control and Prevention's CDC Foundation reports that in the United States nearly 100,000 patient deaths occur annually as a result of hospital-acquired infection.[1] Private organizations, advocates, and public health entities spend countless hours and dollars to provide training and literature on the benefits of hand washing. Yet, many hospital staff continue to disobey this hand-washing protocol. This practice, along with the Semmelweis example, indicates that knowledge alone does not compel people to change their behavior, even when it really matters.

So what makes people with conviction change their behavior? The answer is volition—the purposeful, intentional choice. People choose to change their behavior. Sometimes, the reason for such a decision boils down to dissatisfaction or unhappiness with the status quo; the consequences of not changing are too hurtful or unpalatable. Richard Beckhard and Rubin Harris offer this classic change equation:[2]

dissatisfaction × desirability × practicality > resistance to change

Dissatisfaction is an emotional reaction that is so negative it prevents a person from continuing routine or usual functioning. Although it is a negative experience, dissatisfaction provides a motivation to change. *Desirability* is the reward (the "what's in it for me") for making a change. *Practicality* is the realistic, attainable, and meaningful attributes of the change. A person must be convinced that the change will improve performance, outcomes, and workplace satisfaction.

Influential leaders are highly dissatisfied with the status quo. They are unwilling to allow preventable pain and suffering to continue. They are unwilling to waste precious resources and to settle for second-rate productivity and financial performance. Volition enables dissatisfied leaders to make a choice to bring back meaning and purpose to their work. In addition, volition increases the desirability factor in the change equation. People will likely voluntarily change their behavior if they are told the "why" (the conviction) before they are taught the "what" (convincing) and the "how" (compelling).

Expecting or requiring people to change their behavior (for personal or organizational reasons) is extremely difficult, and some say nearly impossible. Change must come from personal volition that is based on conviction. Being self-aware is imperative in this process. As Gallup research shows, change initiatives in organizations have a high failure rate,[3] because the volitional dimension is often missing from such initiatives. Like conviction, volition comes from deep inside a person, motivating her to do what is necessary to pursue what she perceives to be right for her and others. Unlike conviction, however, volition can be inspired by a negative experience, such as dissatisfaction. For example, a leader cannot rally a person or a team to support her conviction if she cannot show how her proposed change can improve people's lives. But the same leader can encourage the person or the team to rise up and choose change if she outlines how intolerable the current conditions are.

How Influential Leaders Inspire Volition

One key characteristic of influential leaders is their ability to stimulate volition in themselves and among their followers.

They do this by creating a sense of urgency, living a life with purpose, and pursuing excellence.

Sense of Urgency

John Kotter, a well-known change expert, defines urgency as a combination of thinking, attitudes, and behaviors.[4] Urgency is a hyper-alertness and represents a commitment to addressing an important issue that suddenly arises, whether inside or outside of the organization. When organizational leaders are disconnected from the external world, their followers are insulated from external threats to organizational success and thus disconnected from the internal operational elements of the organization, resulting in organizational inertia.

Any organization that lacks a sense of urgency loses to organizational inertia, the status quo, and complacency. Once this condition takes hold, the organization enters a decline and ultimately faces its demise. As a soldier so eloquently stated to his "band of brothers" in 1863 at the Battle of Gettysburg, "Men, I think if we lose this battle, we lose the war." That soldier was Lawrence Joshua Chamberlain, another influential leader whose name may not be familiar to most people. His courage and ability to influence the behavior of his men during the Civil War serve as lessons for us all and frame the core of the army's leadership development: Be-Know-Do. See figure 2-2 for an illustration of how Chamberlain created a sense of urgency among his men.

Life with Purpose

Semmelweis and Chamberlain demonstrate the power of living life with purpose. Discovering your life's purpose stimulates volition, urging you to perform at a higher level. (Performance, rather than success, should be the goal because success is subjective while performance is objective.) When you find this purpose, you also gain the desire to live with sincerity and pursue life goals and objectives that make a difference in your life and the lives of others. High-performing organizations know their fundamental purpose, their mission, and pursue it with a great

Figure 2-2. Sense of Urgency: An Example

When the Civil War began in 1861, Chamberlain, a professor of rhetoric and oratory, could have avoided the entire affair. He had already been approved for an educational sabbatical to England. Against the wishes of his parents, he, along with his younger brother Tom, chose instead to accept a commission in the 20th Maine regiment. His reason for doing so was clear and succinct: "It was the right thing to do."

Chamberlain later wrote of the devastating loss at the Battle of Fredericksburg in 1862, recalling "the bivouac with the dead." All through the night, he stacked bodies of dead Union soldiers in front of his fighting position to shield himself from the rifle fire of Confederate sharpshooters. After this battle, he assumed command of the 20th Maine but had little further involvement in combat until the summer of 1863.

In his account, "Through Blood and Fire at Gettysburg," Chamberlain recalled the bravery of the men who held their position on the Union flank on that fateful day at a place called Little Round Top. His valiant defense of this piece of hallowed ground spawned numerous publications that spoke of the heroism and courage of the men of the 20th Maine regiment. His orders on that day were clear: "You will hold to the last." Hour after hour, the battle raged with the tenacious fighters of the 15th and 47th Alabama regiments. Chamberlain grasped the gravity of his situation. He could not retreat, and his men could not withstand another assault by staying in place. Compounding the enormity of the situation, the men of the 20th Maine had exhausted all their ammunition and faced no opportunity to resupply. In that crisis, through tremendous conviction and resolve that they must prevail, Chamberlain created a great sense of urgency for the remaining members of his beloved regiment: "At that crisis, I ordered the bayonet. The word alone was enough."

How is that for creating a sense of urgency?

Having learned his military tactics by mere observation and experience, Chamberlain led his men on a bayonet charge down the hill, swinging "like a barn door on a hinge" and creating both a frontal assault and a flanking maneuver against the exhausted and now surprised oncoming members of the two Confederate regiments. Understanding the tactical significance of his position, reinforced with a strong personal conviction of the rightness of his cause and ability to create a sense of urgency for his men, Chamberlain led the 20th Maine in its bayonet charge and, in its victory, altered the course of American history. For his courage and tenacity in defense of his position, Chamberlain was awarded the Congressional Medal of Honor and was affectionately named Lion of the Round Top.

sense of urgency. The same adage is true for high-performing individuals, such as influential leaders.

Whether you are on a hand-washing crusade (like Semmelweis) or in a win-or-die battle (like Chamberlain), a clear life purpose enables you to choose the most effective response for any situation without making compromises that will derail your performance.

Pursuit of Excellence

The ultimate end of individual and organizational performance should be excellence, not perfection. The pursuit of excellence has the power to improve outcomes in safety, quality, service, financial prosperity, and growth. The pursuit of perfection, on the other hand, only incites fear. As Vince Lombardi, the legendary football coach, said, "We shall pursue perfection and never attain it. But in our pursuit of perfection we will discover excellence and we will grasp it."

Far too many leaders today motivate their people through fear, barking the prevailing mantra of "innovate, change, reinvent, or die." Not so for influential leaders. Influential leaders support innovation, change, and reinvention, but they know that the worst way to motivate followers to work toward these goals is to threaten them with extinction. Fear is demoralizing, and perfection is unrealistic. Excellence is inspiring. Which leader would you follow? Is it the one who intimidates and pressures you with "If this project doesn't roll out at the end of the year, your department will shut down," or is it the one who approaches you with "I need everyone's help in cutting our expenses. When we reach that goal at the end of the year, I'll find a way to express my thanks to each of you"? As my army training taught me, the ultimate measure of leadership success is excellence, and, in the words of John Wooden, the legendary basketball coach, "excellence is the residual result of continual creation and improvement for its own sake."

Pursuing excellence rouses conviction and volition because it reveals to you the meaningful work you can perform and the life-changing improvements you can achieve.

The Mental Dimension

The mental dimension of self-awareness concerns our own mental models. The mental model is our intellectual and psychological framework for understanding, interpreting, and experiencing the world around us. It includes our attitudes, biases, intuition, insights, preferences, justifications, reasoning, and other cognitive processes. We develop these models over a lifetime (and, sometimes, on the spot), and we rely on them to help us in various ways—from defending ourselves against threats to processing information to dealing with others to making decisions to responding to stimuli.

A mental model is a simple and incomplete representation of a bigger, more complicated idea, and it is based on a self-perceived truth rather than the actual truth. More important, a mental model predicts behavior. For example, some staff may hold as a mental model that taking initiative to change an ineffective process is viewed as insubordination by their managers and supervisors. As a result, these workers are intimidated and are reluctant to engage in any improvement. Similarly, a senior leader's mental model may be that he has already learned and experienced everything there is to know about leadership, and thus he is resistant to continuous development.

Becoming self-aware entails examining our mental models—specifically, how they help or hinder our behaviors and performance. Influential leaders, because they are other-centered and not self-centered, are attuned to their mental models as well as those of their followers. This awareness enables influential leaders to adjust their behavior and to guide others in making necessary changes to their behaviors. Replacing dysfunctional mental models—especially those held and considered functional for a long time—is a daunting task. It is not an overnight undertaking but a careful process that relies on volition (or will), courage, purposeful thinking, and mental toughness and self-discipline.

Figure 2-3 offers self-assessment questions to help you start thinking about your mental patterns in relation to your job, those around you, your behavior, and your performance.

Purposeful Thinking

Ralph Waldo Emerson wrote: "The hardest thing to do in the world is to think well." Many people can agree with this statement, as we often operate daily on *autopilot*—the automatic performance of tasks that requires no reflection. Being on autopilot is a time-saver, especially in an environment like health care that is highly demanding and constantly evolving. Health

Figure 2-3. Try This: Evaluate Your Mental Model

- Before undertaking your current position or career, what assumptions did you hold about the industry, the job, the work, the organization, the workers, or the people being served? How did your assumptions affect your performance and relationships?

- To what extent were these assumptions proven true? To what extent were they found false? What lessons did you learn and do you continue to learn?

- How do you perceive yourself, your performance, your behavior at work, and your colleagues' performance and behavior? Do these perceptions tend to be negative or positive? Have you received feedback or comments that support your perceptions?

- What is your general attitude about teamwork, personal and organizational improvement, change and development initiatives, and management and leadership? To what extent has your mind-set (negative or positive) helped or hampered these factors?

- Are you averse to change, or do you view change as an opportunity? Why? What is your general philosophy about change? How do you gain buy-in from other people about change?

- Do you think before you speak and speak before you act? Why or why not? What is your strategy for communicating and exchanging ideas? Does your strategy work, and why?

- When your team fails to achieve optimal results, what thoughts race through your mind? How do these thoughts affect your team's other and subsequent goals?

care chiefs must continually assess the organization's strategies and market position, managers must continually resolve one crisis after another, clinical staff must continually respond to the medical needs of patients, and support staff must continually tend to the demands of everybody else.

Who has time to think, let alone evaluate their thought processes? Isn't health care work hard enough? These are valid rhetorical questions. But they provide no excuse for the lack of purposeful thinking taking place in health care facilities. Furthermore, such statements only underscore the point that progress in health care delivery and sustainable success in operations are the products of creative and innovative solutions—which are not possible to achieve when everyone is on autopilot.

Often, what separates good leaders from influential leaders is the latter group's tendency to think purposefully. In general, purposeful thinking is the act of quieting the mind and thinking critically. In this context, it is about identifying mental models in an effort to separate functional from dysfunctional thinking and behavior. Purposeful thinking should be positive, focused, and driven by conviction and values.

- *Positive.* Our behaviors are a manifestation of our thoughts (we are what we think). Thus, any negative preconceived notions we have could impair our interactions with others and derail or delay our desired outcome.
- *Focused.* Focus enables our thinking to be specific and direct. If the goal is to eliminate behaviors that harm, then those behaviors and the thoughts that drive them should be named and dealt with one by one. Commitment is a form of focus. Influential leaders who are focused are committed and thus can "tune out" disruptions, distractions, fear, and fatigue.
- *Driven by conviction and values.* Influential leaders think and behave by convictions that are anchored in the right desire, right motive, and right means. "Right" means

appropriate and beneficial for their followers. These leaders consistently examine whether their mental models and behaviors align with their own convictions and the values of the organization.

Influential leaders embrace virtually every life event and adapt their mental patterns to each event to maximize their performance and relationships. Purposeful thinking (and self-awareness as a whole) requires a good dose of courage, a cardinal virtue espoused by ancient Greek philosophers and modern leaders alike. Self-examination reveals a truth that may be difficult to accept, and courage empowers the leader to turn such revelations into insight and then into daily practice.

Mental Toughness and Self-Discipline

Mental toughness is a hallmark character trait of high-level performers. It is a person's determination, resiliency, focus, and control under pressure. Mental toughness is not inherent; it is learned and developed over many years, usually through self-discipline.

Self-discipline is the ability to control impulses and triumph over weaknesses or temptations, especially in moments of stress and uncertainty. Typically, a leader's self-discipline is judged by how he manages his priorities, how he makes personal and professional decisions and choices, and how he conducts himself in front of others.

- *Priority management.* All of us are pressured to do more with less time, to the extent that "being busy" is no longer seen as a pat excuse but an unfortunate reality. The discipline to manage priorities with limited time is invaluable; it requires scheduling the priorities, rather than prioritizing the schedule. Self-disciplined leaders understand the difference between urgent and important tasks, and they have a well-organized system for dealing with each category of tasks along with other nonessential issues that inevitably come up.

- *Personal and professional decisions and choices.* Self-disciplined leaders are known to have orderly, stable lives. Their choices are predictable, and their decisions are prudent. They do not get caught in momentary lapses of judgment, nor do they place themselves in situations that will hurt their reputation or cause others to doubt their values. Their words and actions are always aligned, and their public and private personas are consistent with each other.

- *Conduct.* Observable behavior is a major determinant of self-discipline. For example, in a crisis, a self-disciplined leader responds and reacts calmly; stays focused on the task at hand; offers and seeks solutions proactively; reserves blame and criticism until all facts are in, and keeps them private in the process; and displays genuine concern and care. A self-disciplined leader shows appropriate but not over-the-top (e.g., lashing out, being stoic) emotions. In addition, this leader is a visible presence on all units and is regularly available to all staff, which engenders a mind-set that the leader is accessible.

Without self-discipline, people ultimately succumb to the urges and impulses of their emotions and lose their focus, which in turn damage their reputation and may end their career. Having self-discipline alone does not guarantee that a leader will become an excellent performer, but it is an essential starting point for achieving mental toughness.

Usually associated with athletics, mental toughness is a critical contributor to performance excellence. Mental toughness builds and strengthens your resolve, drowns out doubt and fear, and prepares you for the unanticipated. This kind of focused mental model opens a person up to learning or being "teachable." Being teachable, in turn, provides the following advantages:

1. *A pool of sources, experts, mentors, and colleagues.*
   Health care work—from administration to delivery—is
   a team pursuit; it cannot be carried out in isolation.
   To think otherwise is absurd, because one person's
   knowledge, experience, skills, insight, and talent (no
   matter how great) will never be sufficient for the flow
   of change, challenge, and chaos that hits the organization on an ongoing basis. Many arrogant leaders try to
   function alone, but doing so is a disservice to the organization because it limits everyone's capacity to grow and
   improve. Mentally tough leaders are lifelong learners. As
   such, they develop a wide network of people on whom
   they rely to gain insight and information and with whom
   they exchange advice, strategies, and solutions. This
   circle is diverse, comprising followers, colleagues, leaders from other organizations, professional mentors or
   coaches, and friends. Everyone in this circle benefits
   from the shared learning.

2. *A feedback mechanism.* People who are teachable are
   making a humble and courageous admission: I need to
   improve. In the process of improvement and learning,
   feedback is mandatory. Otherwise, a person will not
   know if she is applying the learning correctly or if she
   is making progress toward her desired goal. Mentally
   tough minds expect and welcome feedback from every
   source of learning, especially challenging situations.

3. *Opportunities for creative thinking.* Creative decision
   making and problem solving is in danger of becoming
   obsolete in today's damage-control mode of health care.
   In times of crisis, proposed solutions are often viewed as
   either/or options, not as pathways to other ideas. Every
   lesson learned, no matter how devastating, offers an
   opportunity for creative exploration, as this quote from
   community planners involved in rebuilding after Hur-
   ricane Katrina supports:[5]

> I think we've got to look beyond ourselves to come up with the most creative way of creating a health care system. [Our] purpose is not just to provide quality, culturally competent health care. [Our] responsibility . . . is to do that, plus engage the healthcare system so [we] can transform it.

Mental toughness is a form of mental programming that enables us to manage our thoughts in such a way that we behave according to our conviction and according to practices that yield high-level performance.

The Connection between Brain and Behavior

In his book, *Get Out of Your Own Way: The Five Keys to Surpassing Everyone's Expectations*, Dr. Robert Cooper argues that a number of interests compete for our brain's attention.[6] This competition and the tension it creates are the reason we have a hard time recognizing our mental patterns and changing our behavior. It seems that our brain, like all of us, is too busy processing information to carefully categorize incoming thoughts and behaviors into functional versus dysfunctional and productive versus unproductive categories. As mentioned in chapter 1, once our brain commits to a certain thinking pattern, that pattern is hard to get rid of and is immediately manifested through our behavior. It is an automatic cause-and-effect phenomenon.

This connection between behavior and the brain explains the process of being on autopilot: The brain makes a one-time choice, and the body enacts the choice for a long time, allowing the brain to avoid having to reflect on or consider any other alternatives. As discussed earlier, being on autopilot is a common approach to a time-limited life. However, when we operate on autopilot, we abdicate personal accountability for our choices, our actions, and their consequences. Worse, it gives us a false sense of reality: We have no control over our performance, processes, and outcomes. Simply stated, being on autopilot takes away our volition. This perception of reality then becomes part of our mental model, discouraging us from taking risks, exploring possibilities, or being innovative. In this sense, we are stuck, unable to break away from the rigid, false structure our brain has created.

Your quest for performance excellence—to be an influential leader—is predicated on you *not* putting your brain on autopilot. You have conviction and volition on your side, so rely on them.

The Role of Conviction and Convincing in Behavior Change

Introduced in chapter 1, the C^4 model components of conviction and convincing are interrelated, much as the brain and behavior are linked. Both conviction and convincing originate in the mind and are the products of a lifetime of experiences, knowledge, insights, wins, and failures.

While the convincing component provides an explanation of how our mental patterns affect our behavior and performance, the conviction component drives us to make the choice to change, to act on what we know. This choice requires courage. When we see, think, and feel with courage, our core values come into focus and our commitment is solidified. We engage and connect with others, rather than isolate ourselves. Conversely, when we choose to see, think, and feel without courage, our impulse takes over and we start to worry, fear, and doubt.

The conviction and convincing components of the C^4 model help you get back in touch with your volition and mental capabilities. They pose questions for self-reflection with the intention of reframing and reprogramming the way you think, make decisions, behave, and interact with others. See the "Applying the C^4 Model" section at the end of the chapter.

Conclusion

Before any real behavior change can take place in our lives, we must use our volition to transform our mind-set to this truth:

Behavior change is possible, and it can enhance our behavior, interactions, and performance. Influential leaders accept this truth, and it is evident in their daily behavior and relationships. What helps in any change effort is self-awareness—a deep understanding of our own thoughts, beliefs, values, strengths and weaknesses, and mental models. Without such self-awareness, we cannot grasp the why (conviction), the what (convincing), and the how (compelling) of change and so will resist change.

The mental toughness and self-discipline necessary to improve performance and behavior do not develop overnight. They are the result of years of purposeful thinking, continuous learning, and living by conviction—activities that require both courage and commitment.

Key Takeaways

- Conviction is a deeply felt belief that guides our thoughts, emotions, choices, biases, responses, and behaviors. Conviction must be supported by volition.

- Volition is the conscious, willful act of making a decision. It explains that what we choose to believe determines how we choose to behave, and vice versa.

- People will likely voluntarily change their behavior if they are told the why (the conviction) before they are taught the what (convincing) and the how (compelling).

- Change must come from personal volition that is based on conviction.

- Influential leaders can stimulate volition in themselves and among followers by creating a sense of urgency, living a life with purpose, and pursuing excellence.

- A sense of urgency is a hyper-alertness and represents a commitment to making something happen to address an important issue that suddenly arises, whether inside or outside of the organization.

- A life with purpose stimulates volition, urging you to perform at a higher level. This purpose gives you the desire to live with sincerity and pursue goals, objectives, activities, and outcomes that make a difference.

- The pursuit of excellence has the power to improve outcomes in safety, quality, service, financial prosperity, and growth. Pursuing excellence rouses conviction and volition because it reveals to you the meaningful work you can perform and the life-changing improvements you can achieve.

- The mental model is our intellectual and psychological framework for understanding, interpreting, and experiencing the world around us. It includes our attitudes, biases, intuition, insights, preferences, justifications, reasoning, and other cognitive processes.

- Influential leaders, because they are other-centered and not self-centered, are attuned to their mental models as well as those of their followers. This awareness enables influential leaders to adjust their behavior and to guide others in making necessary changes to their behaviors.

- Purposeful thinking should be positive, focused, and driven by conviction and values.

- Mental toughness is a person's determination, resiliency, focus, and control under pressure. It is learned and developed over many years, usually through self-discipline.

- Self-discipline is the ability to control impulses and triumph over weaknesses or temptations, especially in moments of stress and uncertainty. Having self-discipline alone does not guarantee that a leader will become an excellent performer, but it is an essential starting point for achieving mental toughness.

- Mental toughness builds and strengthens your resolve, drowns out doubt and fear, and prepares you for the unanticipated. This kind of focused mental model opens a person up to learning or being teachable.

- Functioning on autopilot is a common approach to a time-limited life. However, when we operate on autopilot, we abdicate personal accountability for our choices, our actions, and their consequences. Worse, it gives us a false sense of reality: We have no control over processes and outcomes.

- While the convincing component of the C^4 model provides an explanation of how our mental patterns affect our behavior and performance, the conviction component drives us to make the choice to change, to act on what we know.

Applying the C^4 Model: Volitional (Conviction) and Mental (Convincing)

The following questions are intended to initiate self-examination of how your conviction, volition, and mental model affect your productivity, performance, behavior, and personal and professional relationships. Take the time to think about these questions, and be honest with yourself.

- Make a list of your convictions (e.g., I believe that everyone should be treated fairly and equally). Then answer these two questions for each conviction: (1) How does this conviction translate to my daily behavior? (2) Does this conviction help or hamper my performance and interactions, and how?

- What do you spend most of your free time doing? Is it a reflection of your true passions or beliefs? If not, what are you doing to align your conviction to your activities and pursuits?

- Describe a scenario (at work or at home) in which your conviction was tested and made you doubt everything you knew. Did it strengthen or weaken your volition, and how? What did you learn from that experience?

- Describe a scenario (at work or at home) in which you relied on volition. What did you learn from that experience?

- List instances in which you made a decision on autopilot. What pros and cons did these experiences bring?

- How do you motivate your followers to change or buy into your ideas? Do you create a sense of urgency, inspire them to live purposefully, and coach them in pursuing excellence? What roles do fear and intimidation play in your strategy, and what effects do they have on you, your staff, and morale at the workplace?

- How attuned are you to your followers' needs and wants? To what extent are you familiar with their mental patterns such that you can predict their behavior? How do you display your respect for and trust in them? How do they display their respect for and trust in you? Can you rely on them to assist and support you? Why, or why not?

- Are you teachable? How do you ensure that you continue to learn about yourself, about your work, and about others? What systems are in place for such learning?

- Do you practice purposeful thinking? If so, describe your method. State how this practice has helped you make decisions, respond and react in crises, or improve your interpersonal interactions. If not, what is your thinking approach, and how does it help or hamper you?

- Describe a scenario (at work or at home) in which your mental model conflicted with your behavior or caused problems between you and others. What did you learn from this experience? How did it strengthen or weaken your conviction, and how does it help or hamper your future dealings?

References

1. CDC Foundation, "Hand Washing: A Simple Step to Prevent Hospital Infections," 2009 [http://www.cdcfoundation.org/frontline/articles/2010-03/hand-washing-simple-step-prevent-hospital-infections]. Accessed August 26, 2009.

2. R. Beckhard and R. Harris, "Beckhard and Harris's Change Equation," 2009 [http://www.mindtools.com/pages/article/newPPM_67.htm]. Accessed August 26, 2009.

3. T. Rath and B. Conchie, *Strengths-Based Leadership: Great Leaders, Teams, and Why People Follow* (New York: Gallup Press, 2008, 7–10).

4. J. Kotter, *A Sense of Urgency* (Boston: Harvard Business School Publishing, 2008).

5. B.F. Springgate, C. Allen, C. Jones, S. Lovera, D. Meyers, L. Campbell, L. Palinkas, and K.B. Wells, "Rapid Community Participatory Assessment of Health Care in Post-storm New Orleans." *American Journal of Preventive Medicine* 37, no. 6, suppl. 1 (2009): S237–S243.

6. R. Cooper, *Get Out of Your Own Way: The Five Keys to Surpassing Everyone's Expectations* (New York: Crown Business, 2006, 3).

3

The Emotional Dimension

Your emotional memory provides a high gear
that stimulates forceful self-regulated action
for making new choices that move you toward
what really matters in your life.

—Robert K. Cooper, author and leadership expert

Human emotions are as complex as they are varied. In a span of one day, we all experience a significant number of emotional highs and lows. An average person in a high-stress environment, like health care, may experience even more. Emotions do not take a break, even when we need a break. They are always present, influencing our and others' behavior, performance, and interactions.

Being aware of your emotions means being able to manage them. While you can stimulate, inspire, and detect emotions in others, you cannot control their emotions. Only they can manage theirs, and you, yours. Influential leaders are adept at handling their emotions, and this competency is useful for everyone they interact with. It sets them free from the negative energies stirred up by emotional interactions. It places them in a position to model emotionally balanced behavior. More important, it enables them to be responsive to others' needs, which is a primary contributor to employee engagement.

In this chapter, we explore emotional self-awareness and the compelling component of the C^4 model. Specifically, we explain what emotional awareness is, what impact it has on employee engagement and performance, and what approaches help us better manage our emotions.

What Is Emotional Awareness?

Twenty years ago, the idea of emotions having an impact on personal and professional success, productivity, and performance was given a name: *emotional intelligence.* Emotional intelligence (EI), first defined in an article by psychologists Peter Salovey and John Mayer, is "the subset of social intelligence that involves the ability to monitor one's own and others' feelings and emotions, to discriminate among them and to use this information to guide one's thinking and actions."[1] Popularized and expanded by Daniel Goleman, EI (or EQ for emotional quotient) has remained relevant in the fields of organizational development and leadership development.

Emotional awareness operates under the same principles as EI. Its message is simple: When you are emotionally aware, you are conscious of others' emotions and are more able to bring out the best of their behavior and performance. When you are emotionally unaware, you cannot relate well to others and engage them, and you are more likely to cause dissatisfaction, conflict, and dysfunction.

Impact on the Workforce

A leader's emotional awareness is important because employees (or followers) relate to their leaders on an emotional level in several ways. First, how employees *feel* (e.g., awed, intimidated, indifferent, impressed) about their leader influences the way they do their job and the way they behave on the job. This feeling extends to whether they stay or leave the organization and whether they act as ambassadors (or proud advocates) of the organization. Second, a leader's words, attitudes, and behavior stir up various (negative and/or positive) emotions in employees. Even followers who manage their emotions well can be affected by this emotional energy. It is this inadvertent or unconscious control that leaders have over the emotional state of their followers that can distort the dynamic between management and employees, creating dysfunctions. For example, a leader who has a fondness for telling corny jokes may amuse some employees but annoy and frustrate the rest. This reaction could lead to a loss of respect for the leader, especially if the employees cannot ask the boss to cut out or cut down the jokes. Third, a leader's professional decisions and strategies can be taken personally by some employees and thus meet an unexpected emotional response. In a financial downturn, everyone is nervous about losing his or her job; any change to current practices may be misconstrued as economic instability and can stimulate anger and fear.

Emotional Triggers

Emotionally aware leaders understand their own (and, by extension, their employees') emotional triggers. Emotional triggers are people, events, conditions, or experiences that arouse intense negative reactions. Incompetence, micromanagement, constantly missing or incomplete information, arrogant and superior attitude, lack of communication, and excessive number of unproductive meetings are just some of the emotional triggers at play in the workplace. Once triggered, an emotional reaction may stir up other negative memories and negate any positive experiences.

Close observation is the best way to learn about emotional triggers. Pay strict attention to everything that is going on during an emotional interaction, including your own reaction. Immediately after the episode has passed, note your answers to the following questions:

- What triggered the event? (Write down a summary of what happened. Include background information, such as past discussions, responses, and compromises. Be detailed so that you can find cause-and-effect relationships among the specifics.)

- What emotions were felt and displayed? (It is easy to answer this question for yourself, but judge others' emotions by how they acted. Often, body language is louder than actual words, especially for people who react passively. Make a list of your own and others' emotions, then compare them. Are they similar or different, and why?)
- What words were exchanged? (These words are informative. In the heat of the moment, people are generally honest about their feelings and thoughts. If you listen carefully, you will find out a lot about what is working and what is not working.)
- How quickly did the situation escalate, and how long did it last? (This time frame is important because it indicates the depth of the emotions felt or length of time they have been repressed. It could also signal how difficult or easy it will be to repair the relationship and correct the emotional trigger.)
- What are the emotional consequences of the event for you and for the others? (Make a list of the emotions you and others displayed afterward—embarrassed, angry, sad, relieved, regretful, and so on. Compare them. Are they similar or different, and why?)

Over time, observing these emotional reactions will give you insight into your own and your employees' emotional patterns. Then, you can use this knowledge to better manage your emotions by changing your mental models, relying on your convictions and volition. By managing your own emotions, you are being mindful and considerate of others' emotions and avoiding their emotional triggers.

Emotions respond to how you think about an event or a situation in your life. How you choose to remember previous life events, and the emotions associated with those events, feeds how you will respond or react to current and future situations.

Characteristics of Emotionally Aware Leaders

Authenticity, humility, honesty, and courage are hallmark traits of influential leaders, and they all can be attributed to the leader's emotional awareness. Additional emotionally aware characteristics of influential leaders are discussed in this section.

Mental Presence

Being mentally present reflects a conscious decision to pay full attention (physically, mentally, and emotionally) to everything that is occurring around you. This mental presence enables us to focus, observe, learn, listen, form an opinion, and develop insight. Equally important, it prevents us from saying or doing anything that could trigger an emotional reaction in others. Influential leaders are mentally present at all times. This attention allows them to think before they act but act before it is too late.

Emotional Control

Influential leaders take care in what they say and do because they know they are being watched all the time. During a crisis or a contentious event, employees may even be expecting an emotional reaction from their leaders.

Having emotional control does not mean repressing feelings. It means making a conscious effort to stay focused, composed, and even-tempered. No one benefits from a leader whose first reaction to a bad situation is to scream at everyone around her or one who sobs in public when he is overwhelmed. Conversely, no one benefits from a leader who is so emotionally closed up that she cannot show compassion, affection, or joy when necessary or appropriate.

Again, employees relate to their leaders on an emotional level. So a leader's mood, feeling, attitude, and behavior have a significant impact on those of employees. A leader's lack of emotional control could leave employees physically, mentally, and emotionally drained and could encourage them to disengage.

Inspiration

Self-awareness of your volition, mental models, and emotions is the strongest foundation you have for inspiring others. When you are self-aware, you are sympathetic to the plight of others and you are likely to want to make a difference in their lives. In addition, you understand and thus avoid your own emotional triggers, and that gives you insight into people's emotional patterns—what makes them happy, sad, angry, and so on.

Being inspirational is second nature to self-aware, influential leaders. They inspire others with their words, actions, behavior, character, experiences, and self-confidence and self-control. Often, these leaders do not even know they are inspirational. They do the right things because they are compelled to do so. Unknown to them, their display of caring, compassion, mental toughness, and integrity serves as an inspiration to those around them.

Responsiveness to Concerns and Needs

The common employee question "How will *(fill in the blank)* affect my job?" is emotion driven. It implies worry about employees' livelihood, not an intellectual interest in the job dynamics. Emotionally aware leaders are responsive to these feelings. For example, in a crisis situation or when encountering a fallout from any of their decisions, these leaders are courageous and calm:

- They minimize panic and confusion by providing comprehensive and candid information.
- They offer alternatives and resources.
- They display knowledge, resolve, and control.
- They show empathy and willingness to help.
- They make themselves visible and available to answer any questions and listen to comments. They encourage employees to contact them directly, not their assistants or lower-level managers.
- They refuse to take personally any employee frustrations, and they show respect for these feelings.
- They do not participate in or give credence to negative discussions and rumors.

In addition, emotionally aware leaders actively seek information to understand and respond to the various needs of their employees. Often, these needs are not communicated clearly and are expressed as laments—for example, "I feel so out of the loop" (need to be included) or "No one listens to my ideas" (need to feel respected and valued). An emotionally aware leader hears between the lines, so to speak. She knows that all employees (including herself) have the same basic needs, but the degree of importance given to each need varies from person to person and from situation to situation. For example, one person feels stifled because she has to give weekly updates to her boss, but she feels grateful that her boss is always available to help her. While this person needs to feel independent most of the time, she needs to feel supported all of the time.

Needs of the Generationally Diverse Workforce

Four generations of people make up the current workforce in the United States—silent or traditional (born before 1946), baby boomer (born approximately between 1946 and 1964), generation X (born approximately between 1965 and 1979), and millennial or generation Y (born approximately 1980 and after). All the generations share strong work ethics and workplace needs. They all want work that is meaningful and that adds purpose to their lives.

The following excerpt from "How to Manage the Four Generations in Today's Workplace," by Lynn Lieber, is a succinct description of each generation's needs and motivations.[3]

Traditionalists need respect.
They are motivated by acknowledgment of their historical experience and expertise. They maintain an attitude of commitment and endurance and make personal sacrifices for the greater good. Their professional relationships are formal and reinforce workplace hierarchies.

Baby boomers need success.
They view money as evidence of social status. They are motivated by material gain and professional advancement. Although driven, as individuals, boomers promote collaborative efforts and prefer business decisions to be made by consensus. Boomers believe in the importance of following historical precedents and take a process-oriented approach to their work.

Rather than gather test scores, the employer should conduct training in a manner in which it will be able to show that the employee spent a sufficient amount of time in the training, had to interact with the materials, and agreed to abide by the employer's policies.

Generation X needs autonomy.
Supervisors should provide feedback, not give orders. Generation X employees are motivated by professional growth and flexibility in their work. They work independently, believe in personal responsibility, and struggle to fit work into their lives. For Generation X, precedent is superseded by what is pragmatic, and its members' informal approach undermines workplace hierarchy and positional authority.

Generation Y needs validation.
Generation Y employees seek to contribute to society and to make a difference. Flexibility and the opportunity to pursue personal growth are highly motivational to Generation Y employees. Generation Y believes in its own hype and maintains a self-absorbed and inflated self-image—even in the face of failure or rejection. Generation Y expects equality, and its members consider everyone from the CEO to the mail clerk as their peers. Their casual approach to work and social interactions reflects their desire for immediate recognition on a professional and personal level.

Employee needs fall under the Two-Factor Theory, also known as the Motivation-Hygiene Theory, a framework developed by psychologist Frederick Herzberg. According to this theory, employees have two kinds of needs: hygiene (e.g., good salary and benefits, job security, safe workplace) and motivation (e.g., job growth, feeling of accomplishment, recognition). In his research, Herzberg found that "motivators were the primary cause of satisfaction, and hygiene factors the primary cause of unhappiness on the job."[4] In other words, when employees are not satisfied with their job, they say it is because of hygiene factors (e.g., low pay, bad boss), but when they are satisfied they say it is because of motivation factors (e.g., fulfilling work).

Herzberg's theory, which he introduced in 1959, is still relevant today. Motivation factors are based on employees' emotional connection to their work. These factors continue to be included on many (if not all) lists of employee demands from their organizations, such as the list in figure 3-1. Gallup research on strengths-based leadership (see chapter 2) indicates that the more people feel that their emotional needs are being met, the more energized, engaged, and passionate they are about their performance, productivity, and overall commitment to the mission and vision of the organization.[5]

Many leaders are unaware of the needs and concerns of their workforce. Unmet needs produce strong negative feelings, such as resentment. These employees become complainers, cynics, and fault finders. They resist change, and they disengage from the culture and all initiatives. They "just work here," and only until they can find another job—that is their prevalent

Figure 3-1.   Seven Emotions-Based Employee Needs

Research in human resources and talent management has identified the following employee needs that, when met, lead to high levels of engagement and retention.[6]

1. *Inclusion and belonging.* People have a fundamental need to be in a healthy, supportive relationship. At work, this includes being part of the discussion and decision making that affects their job. "No one wins alone," so the saying goes, and no one wants to work alone, either.

2. *Appreciation and recognition.* We all have an emotional need to be appreciated for who we are as a person as well as for our gifts, talents, and abilities. Meaningful and effective recognition programs have three types of acknowledgment: (1) day to day, which may include a simple pat on the back, kind words, or a thank-you card; (2) informal, which may include a "thank-you gram" or a certificate of appreciation from the department; and (3) formal, which may include a notice in organizational media (such as the intranet and Web site, employee newsletter, and bulletin boards) or a luncheon or banquet.

3. *Challenge and achievement.* Having challenging work provides us the opportunity to use the best of our gifts, talents, and abilities. Data suggest that every day a vast majority of people go to a job and hate it simply because it does not challenge them mentally or give them an opportunity for achievement.[7]

mind-set. Failing that outcome, they will demand more money, more benefits, or unusual work arrangements. Leaders must realize that these negative behaviors are the employees' way of compensating for the emotional fulfillment they are missing from the job. Leaders cannot throw money at this problem, as that solution will only bring more difficulties.

Commitment to Employee Engagement

Actual organizational results show that employee engagement is a key contributor to improved operations,[9] financial growth, and enhanced management-workforce relationships.[10] In addition, "organizations that have a high level of employee engagement are going to have workers that are more productive; they

Figure 3-1.   (Continued)

4. *Trust and accountability.* Productive relationships cannot exist without trust. We need to know that we can count on others and that we are all playing on a level field. A Gallup study, conducted from 2005 to 2008, on why people follow their leaders found that trust was the number one trait employees seek from their superiors. Trust was followed by compassion, stability, and hope.[8]

5. *Growth and learning.* Continuing education and training dollars seem to be the first sacrificial offering in any cost-cutting initiative. But learning and improving our skills are fundamental emotions-based needs. We feel happy when we expand our knowledge, and we are thankful and more committed to those who provide such an opportunity.

6. *Power and control.* Everyone wants to be empowered enough to control their own work processes and to have a say in how those processes should change. No one appreciates saying or hearing "I only work here. It's not up to me." It is demoralizing and discouraging.

7. *Meaning and purpose.* People want and need to know that their daily work contributes to a larger effort, one that is more valuable than making money. Health care work has intrinsic value, meaning, and purpose. The irony, however, is that countless health care workers (including professionals) trudge off to their jobs every day not recognizing that what they do has so much meaning. They are mentally overwhelmed, physically exhausted, and emotionally depleted by the constant stress and demands of their job.

work harder; they're happier; they stay longer; they come to work every day—and the study showed that recognition is one of the key pieces of the puzzle that lead to people being happy and engaged in an organization."[11]

Employee engagement as a whole is a program of getting the workforce enthusiastic about and involved in their work, the organization, and higher levels of performance. While employee satisfaction is still a goal for many organizations, it is no longer sufficient to achieve peak performance in an economically constrained health care environment[12] that employs *knowledge workers,* a term traditionally reserved for information technology personnel, architects, coders, and researchers but that has now come to mean all employees, including frontline staff.[13]

Gone are the days when a paycheck, the employee-of-the-month award, and a gold watch at retirement were sufficient motivators for people to perform at their best or to remain loyal and dedicated to the organization. Employees today seek to work for a company and leaders with whom that they feel proud to be associated and who treat them like active contributors, not passive producers. They want to work for leaders who appreciate the value they add and rely on their passions and talents to every extent possible.

Influential leaders engage their employees in various ways, including the following:

- Communicating regularly
- Sharing appropriate information
- Soliciting feedback
- Rewarding and recognizing good work
- Responding to personal and professional needs
- Providing timely and adequate resources and guidance
- Inviting them into decision-making, problem-solving, and brainstorming processes

All of these tactics require emotional awareness. How do you engage your workforce? See figure 3-2 to assess yourself.

Figure 3-2. Try This: Assess the Level of Engagement in Your Organization

Answer "yes" or "no" to the following statements:

- The vast majority of the workforce has more talent, energy, creativity, motivation, and achievement desire than their respective positions allow or than the leadership uses.

- The level of employee engagement in my organization is not as high as it could be: Workers could be more productive; they could work harder; they could be happier; they could stay longer; they could come to work every day.

- Leaders in my organization mismanage the power of emotions. (This mismanagement can lead to employee physical and mental health issues if leaders' emotional responses are consistently negative, and it can even contribute to increased cost of health benefits and workers' compensation claims.)

Assessing the Compelling Dimension

Emotional awareness is the compelling dimension of the C^4 model. This dimension assesses how emotions affect behavior and how behavior, in turn, affects people. In other words, the compelling dimension seeks to find out which leadership emotions compel followers to connect and engage and which compel them to turn away.

Interview any group of employees and you will hear a common description of an ineffective leader's behavior: not approachable, poor listener, poor communicator, self-centered, egocentric, not trustworthy, mean, rude, subject to mood swings, just to name a few traits. How would you and those around you characterize your behavior? Answer the short assessment questionnaire in figure 3-3, and then ask several of your colleagues and staff to complete it. Choose people with whom you have had a long-term relationship to ensure a better assessment. Assure them that their opinions matter and that their participation will have no repercussions. Last, arrange for a third party to collect or receive the completed questionnaires;

Figure 3-3. Emotional Awareness Questionnaire

Check off the best answer for each row. Answer the statements as honestly as possible; ask yourself "What do I really feel about this person?" If you are completing the questionnaire for someone else, do not write your name on this form.

Name of person being assessed: _____

  1. Is self-centered and disregards the feelings of others
     Yes___ No ___ Occasionally___

  2. Is a good listener and a wise teacher
     Yes___ No ___ Occasionally___

  3. Seeks the counsel and opinions of staff and colleagues before making important departmental or organizational decisions
     Yes___ No ___ Occasionally___

  4. Is calm and composed but responsive during a crisis or change effort
     Yes___ No ___ Occasionally___

  5. Talks with staff about their needs, goals, and problems
     Yes___ No ___ Occasionally___

  6. Complains about or procrastinates on dealing with difficult issues
     Yes___ No ___ Occasionally___

  7. Welcomes/invites colleagues and staff to provide feedback on his or her emotions and behavior
     Yes___ No ___ Occasionally___

  8. Is emotionally volatile, physically intimidating, and verbally abusive
     Yes___ No ___ Occasionally___

  9. Is involved in confrontation, conflict, and strife
     Yes___ No ___ Occasionally___

 10. Rewards and recognizes accomplishments
     Yes___ No ___ Occasionally___

Please offer three suggestions to help this person improve his or her behavior.

1. _____

2. _____

3. _____

this step will ease the participant's mind that his or her involvement is confidential. Once the answers are collected, including yours, compare the responses.

Avoid getting defensive about people's assessment of your behavior and emotional display, especially if you do not agree. Feeling defensive is a natural and common reaction, even from the emotionally aware. The difference is that emotionally aware leaders can acknowledge their gut reactions and quickly prevent a possible emotional meltdown. They are aware that negative responses are counterproductive to peak performance.

Determining Your Own Behavioral Style

Emotions are our response to our thinking and mental patterns (discussed in chapter 2). Our mental patterns, in turn, predict our behavioral style. And our behavioral style can stir up emotions in others.

Behavioral style, or social/communication style, is the way we conduct ourselves in front of other people, particularly in the workplace. Are you friendly and warm? Are you reserved? Are you assertive? Are you in full control? Your behavioral style (which is different from personality) either attracts or repels other people, and vice versa. Sometimes we cannot articulate why we like or dislike someone's behavior, because these types of preferences are unconscious.[14]

Four categories of behavioral styles are generally recognized. Note that each researcher assigns different names to the attributes:

- analytical, driver, amiable, and expressive (developed by Larry Wilson Learning System)
- thinker, feeler, intuitor, and sensor (developed by Carl Jung)
- thinker, director, relator, and socializer (developed by Tony Alessandra)
- dominance, influence, steadiness, and conscientiousness (developed by William Moulton Marston)

To better illustrate the concept of behavioral style, following is a brief description of the four categories, using the names from the first bullet point above:

1. *Analytical.* An analytical person is more responsive than assertive, attentive to facts, unemotional, extremely precise, detail oriented, and not fond of small talk.
2. *Driver.* A driver is assertive, interrupts conversation, answers quickly, seeks out key facts, has low levels of empathy, and is extremely task focused.
3. *Amiable.* An amiable person is a good listener, responsive, people focused, and friendly. This person seeks to understand and thrives on building relationships.
4. *Expressive.* An expressive person is enthusiastic and friendly, talks a lot and talks fast, loves to tell stories to convey points, can be loud, seeks to grasp concepts, is assertive, has high levels of empathy, and is people focused.

All of us have a dominant style, but we also have habits that fall into the other three categories. Each style has its strengths and weaknesses, an important consideration in team formation. When building a team, you should include people with different behavioral styles because each style contributes to the team dynamics and team goals. In addition, homogeneity in style is insufficient to tackle the diverse issues and situations the team will confront. (Team dynamics are discussed in chapter 4.)

Identifying your own and being aware of others' behavioral style contribute to your leadership success in several ways. First, this recognition improves your interaction and communication with others. For example, if you know someone has an analytical style, you will adjust the way you talk and act to avoid triggering an emotional reaction in that person so that your interaction with that person accomplishes its goal. Second, it allows you to showcase or model (and thus teach) the combination of behavioral styles that works best. Third, it gives you an opportunity to play to your strength, a performance strategy discussed in chapter 1.

Many behavioral style assessment tools are available in the marketplace. One such tool is the Profiles Performance Indicator™, developed by Profiles International; for more information about this tool, go to http://www.profilesinternational.com/product_ppi.aspx.

Developing Your Emotional Awareness

TRACOM Group, a human resources and talent management firm, suggests the following approaches for developing your emotional awareness, all of which require self-discipline:[15]

1. *Know yourself.* Recognize that your brain is the source of your emotions and behavior. Complete self-awareness (comprising your volition, mental models, and emotional responses) enables you to find the internal causes, consequences, and fixes to every situation you encounter externally.

2. *Control yourself.* The next time you experience an emotion, pay full attention to it. Identify (to yourself and quietly) the emotion you are experiencing, and describe in detail its physical and psychological effects on you. This exercise forces you to think and pause before you let the emotion speak or act for you. In the heat of the moment, controlling one's emotions is difficult, but constant practice of this exercise will slow down your reaction time.

3. *Manage yourself.* Keep your focus—that is the first step to managing emotions. Always know what is most important to you (e.g., accomplishing goals, following your convictions, making a difference in people's lives), and then think about the negative consequences your emotions and behavior can have on what you value most.

4. *Enable yourself.* Do not tolerate other people's bad behavior. Teach them how you want and need to be treated; this is best done in the form of a direct request, such as "Please lower your voice" or "Please let me finish my point." By not accepting inappropriate exchanges and attitudes, you are setting clear boundaries. If you do not enable yourself, you will become bitter and resentful about the poor way you are treated, and ineffective communication, conflict, and degraded workplace performance will be the ultimate outcomes.

Conclusion

Many extremely talented and skilled managers fail because they lack the emotional awareness necessary to compel the workforce to deliver high levels of performance. Your influence as a leader will not increase if you lack emotional competency, regardless of your technical abilities and innate talents.

The old adage "Leave your [emotional] baggage at the door" has never been realistic, reasonable, or responsible for leaders to espouse. Influential leaders know that emotions play a part in how people find value, meaning, and purpose in their work. Influential leaders create a culture or an environment that acknowledges and responds to the emotional needs of the workforce. More important, influential leaders model emotionally aware behaviors that inspire, energize, and engage followers. Collaboration, the topic of part II, is not possible without emotional awareness.

As a leader, you are in a unique position to make a difference in people's lives. Use the conviction, convincing, and compelling dimensions of the C^4 model to understand and manage your volition, mental model, and emotions.

Key Takeaways

- Emotions are our response to our thinking and mental patterns (discussed in chapter 2). Only you can manage your emotions, and others theirs. But you can influence others' emotions because your behavior reflects your own.

- Employees (or followers) relate to their leaders on an emotional level. How employees *feel* about their leader influences the way they do their job and the way they behave on the job.

- When you are emotionally aware, you are conscious of others' emotions and are more able to bring out the best of their behavior and performance. When you are emotionally unaware, you cannot relate well to others and engage them, and you are more likely to cause resentment, dissatisfaction, conflict, and dysfunction.

- Emotional triggers are people, events, conditions, or experiences that arouse intense negative reactions. Once triggered, an emotional reaction may stir up other negative memories and negate any positive experiences. Close observation is the best way to learn about emotional triggers.

- Emotional control means making a conscious effort to stay focused, composed, and even-tempered.

- Unmet needs produce strong negative feelings, such as resentment. Employee needs that lead to high levels of engagement and retention include (1) inclusion and belonging, (2) appreciation and recognition, (3) challenge and achievement, (4) trust and accountability, (5) growth and learning, (6) power and control, and (7) meaning and purpose.

- Employee satisfaction is still a goal for many organizations, but it is no longer sufficient to achieve peak performance in an economically constrained health care environment that employs knowledge workers.

- Employees today seek to work for a company and for leaders with whom they feel proud to be associated and who treat them like active contributors, not passive producers. They want to work for leaders who appreciate the value they add and who rely on their passions and talents to every extent possible.

- Emotional awareness is the compelling dimension of the C⁴ model. This dimension assesses how emotions affect behavior and how behavior, in turn, affects people. It seeks to find out which leadership emotions compel followers to connect and engage and which compel them to turn away.

- Behavioral style, or social/communication style, is the way we conduct ourselves in front of other people. Your behavioral style either attracts or repels other people, and vice versa.

- When building a team, you should include people with different behavioral styles because one style is insufficient to tackle the diverse issues and situations the team will confront.

- Many extremely talented and skilled managers fail because they lack the emotional awareness necessary to compel the workforce to deliver high levels of performance. Your influence as a leader will not increase if you lack emotional competency, regardless of your technical abilities and innate talents.

Applying the C⁴ Model: Emotional (Compelling)

The following questions are intended to initiate self-examination of how you display emotions through your behavior and what effects your emotions have on your employees. Take the time to think about these questions, and be honest with yourself.

- How do you view people (including your staff, colleagues, and the workforce in general)? How do you exhibit that view in your daily interactions?

- What is your initial emotional reaction to the following: unexpected delays; unforeseen outcomes or complications;

poor or marginal financial, clinical, and operational results; events that taint the reputation of the organization and its employees? How would your staff answer this question about you?

- What do you hear people say about your temper, disposition, and behavioral style? How well or poorly does your style complement or work with the styles of those around you? If you have received negative feedback, what steps have you taken to improve or alter your style and behavior?

- What do you think people say about you behind your back? Are you comfortable with this image? Why, or why not?

- How often do you *feel* sincerely appreciated, and how often do you express sincere appreciation? What formal and informal reward and recognition programs are in place in your organization? What feedback do you receive about these programs? Are employees involved in creating these programs? If so, how?

- To what extent do you engage your employees? What types of decisions and problems are they allowed to participate in? What kind of encouragement do they receive to get involved? If none, why? What is your view on employee engagement as a whole?

- How would your staff react if you went to work today and announced your retirement? Imagine your last day at work. Imagine it in detail, including the staff celebrations. What will your staff say about your tenure as a leader? What will they remember the most about their interactions with you? What legacy will you leave behind? Consider this anecdote as you think about this question:

   One seasoned nurse manager occasionally buys lunch for her staff to express her appreciation and gratitude for the hard work her staff put into their jobs. But when things go wrong (which, in her mind, is often), the manager quickly loses her temper and starts blaming and belittling her entire department. She has a tendency to scream, slam doors, publicly criticize minor infractions, and give people the silent treatment. Her employees dread the lunches she throws, because they know she does not mean the sentiments behind them. On the day the manager announces her retirement, her staff goes out for "happy hour" to celebrate without her.

References

1. P. Salovey and J. Mayer, "Emotional Intelligence," *Journal of Imagination, Cognition and Personality* 9, no. 3 (1989–1990): 185–211.

2. S. Covey, *The 7 Habits of Highly Effective People,* rev. ed. (New York: Free Press, 2004).

3. L. Lieber, "How to Manage the Four Generations in Today's Workplace," January 2010 [http://www.workplaceanswers.com/Company/News-Events/WPA-in-the-News/HR–Managing-Four-Generations-Workplace]. Accessed September 3, 2010.

4. F. Herzberg, "One More Time: How Do You Motivate Employees?" *Harvard Business Review* (September–October 1987): 9 [http://www.sph.ukma.kiev.ua/images/Seminar_4_One_More_Time_How_Do_You_Motivate_Employees%20(Herzberg).pdf]. Accessed August 30, 2010.

5. T. Rath and B. Conchie, *Strengths-Based Leadership: Great Leaders, Teams, and Why People Follow* (New York: Gallup Press, 2008, 82–83).

6. J.E. Glaser and C. Jones, "Meeting People's Needs: You Can Create a Needs-Intelligent Workplace," *Leadership Excellence* 25, no. 3 (2008): 13–14.

7. Ibid.

8. Rath and Conchie, *Strengths-Based Leadership.*

9. M. Nolan, "Improving Patient Satisfaction in Hospitals with Employee Engagement," 2009 [http://ezinearticles.com/?Improving-Patient-Satisfaction-in-Hospitals-With-Employee-Engagement&id=2709399]. Accessed September 3, 2010.

10. R. Tomcanin, "Improving Employee Satisfaction and Engagement at Your Hospital: 11 Leadership Best Practices from John Singerling, COO of Palmetto Health Richland," *Hospital Review,* 2009 [http://www.beckershospitalreview.com/news-analysis/improving-employee-satisfaction-and-engagement-at-your-hospital-11-leadership-best-

practices-from-john-singerling-coo-of-palmetto-health-richland.
html]. Accessed September 3, 2010.

11. D. Hartley, "Appreciating Employees Can Do Wonders for Engage-
    ment, ROI," *Talent Management*, October 2009 [http://www.talent
    mgt.com/talent.php?pt=a&aid=1099]. Accessed January 8, 2010.

12. *Talent Management*, "Kenexa's WorkTrends Annual Report Offers
    Guidance on Increasing Workforce Performance," *Talent Manage-
    ment*, October 2009 [http://www.talentmgt.com/industry_news/
    2009/October/5065/index.php]. Accessed January 8, 2010.

13. J. Hagel III and J. Seely Brown, "Are All Employees Knowledge
    Workers?" April 2010 [http://blogs.hbr.org/bigshift/2010/04/are-
    all-employees-knowledge-wo.html]. Accessed September 3, 2010.

14. D. Jensen, "Behavioral Style: Understanding Communication Styles
    Can Advance Your Relationships—and Your Career Prospects," *Sci-
    ence*, 2001 [http://sciencecareers.sciencemag.org/career_magazine/
    previous_issues/articles/2001_03_16/noDOI.4520392953582625
    382]. Accessed September 8, 2010.

15. B. Schwierterman, "Skip the Mirror," *Leadership Excellence* 26, no. 1
    (2009): 17.

PART II

What Is Collaboration?

Unity is strength. . . .
[W]hen there is teamwork and collaboration,
wonderful things can be achieved.
—Mattie Stepanek, poet

The second principle of influential leadership is collaboration. It is the duty of influential leaders to exercise this principle. While self-awareness drives individual performance, collaboration drives organizational performance. Collaboration takes place when two or more parties come together to realize a common goal. In health care, that goal varies—from improving clinical outcomes to developing an innovative service or program to meeting and exceeding patient expectations to increasing the organization's market share to creating a collaborative culture. Collaboration enables the accomplishment of more and greater results.

As mentioned earlier in this book, no one can "do" health care alone. However, the historical operating model in health care (still practiced today) encourages independent achievements, especially in medicine, where an excellent physician is hailed as a "rock star" but the valuable contributions of committed nurses and other supporting caregivers are minimized. One unfortunate consequence of this outdated mind-set is competition. Competition is the antithesis of collaboration. It discourages the sharing of information and resources, promotes a "me first" mentality, and ignores the basic rules of civility, all of which shift focus away from the needs of patients.

The root cause for the failure to collaborate effectively in health care is bad thinking that leads to bad behavior. In health care this incivility is damaging to professional relationships, to patient care, and to the bottom line. The challenge, then, for collaborative-minded leaders is to transform a competitive environment into a collaborative culture. This undertaking requires the leader to be self-aware and to harness the behavioral competencies of influential leaders.

Collaboration has two imperatives: trust and accountability. Known as the heart and soul of collaboration, trust and accountability enable collaboration to form and move forward. Trust and accountability also power the three traits of collaboration: (1) effective communication, (2) cooperative attitude, and (3) integrated team. Part II examines the two imperatives as well as the three traits of collaboration. In addition, part II discusses the conforming dimension of the C^4 model and explains how it assesses a team's level of collaboration.

I was privileged to be part of a collaboration to transform an organizational culture, and the outcome of the group's efforts is documented in a 1997 Joint Commission publication titled *Doing the Right Things Right.*[1] All the member organizations of this collaboration desired to achieve their clinical, financial, and operational objectives; to recruit highly talented people; and to maintain focus on their mission, vision, and values. Yet, with all the "right stuff" these organizations implemented, their overall performance still languished or remained average. In fact, they enjoyed only conditional Joint Commission accreditation.

This collaboration not only was a positive learning experience for all the representatives of the member organizations (myself included) but also was a successful effort. Within a matter of three months, our organizations (and, by extension, our collaboration) were receiving accolades for achieving some of the most dramatic cultural transformations ever recorded by The Joint Commission.

In the following chapters, I share the general lessons (not specific details) I learned from this collaboration. Before proceeding, I want to emphasize two points. First, the collaboration work itself was fulfilling and a lot of fun, even though, in the case at hand, we were operating amid a stressful mandate to immediately fix our respective but similar crises. The energy, passion, excitement, and enthusiasm were pervasive among the group. The joy and thrill we felt each time we achieved a goal were experienced at a higher level than each of us would have felt had we accomplished those goals on our own. Second, the experience left in me the desire to re-create it in every organization of which I become a part. This collaboration revived my conviction to make a difference in people's lives. It made me want to recommit myself to leadership and to performance excellence.

Consequently, the need to create cultures of collaboration is self-evident. The health care system in general has spent countless hours and dollars on methods, programs, and systems to improve safety, quality, and service—but with marginal improvements to these areas. The attributes of one individual are no longer sufficient to drive high levels of performance, for modern health care is too complex. The technical burden and knowledge requirements exceed the capacity of any individual to overcome alone. "We are not omniscient or all powerful," writes Atul Gawande. He continues: "Even with advanced technology our mental and physical powers are limited."[2]

Ironically, advances in technology that are often touted as the panacea for improving health care safety and quality have only provided opportunity for more human error to occur. Better human behavior—guided by influential leadership, executed within a culture of collaboration, and mindful of the C^4 model—is our best hope for improving performance and preventing harm to patients.

References

1. The Joint Commission, *Doing the Right Things Right* (Oakbrook Terrace, IL: The Joint Commission, 1997).
2. A. Gawande, *The Checklist Manifesto—How to Get Things Right* (New York: Metropolitan Books, 2009, 8).

4

Collaboration: The Duty of the Influential Leader

The most useful person in the world today is the man or woman who knows how to get along with other people.
—Stanley C. Allyn, president of NCR

Collaboration is a partnership between people and/or groups intended to generate a product or achieve a singular objective that is mutually beneficial to all parties involved. Collaboration tends to move forward any kind of work or goal faster than any other approach because it is powered by the skills, knowledge, expertise, experience, and insight of many people, not just one. It is particularly critical in service industries, including health care, because the needs and demands in these industries are complex and filled with consequences. In a laboratory, for example, a "simple" blood test involves multiple staff, processes, and knowledge areas. All of these units or players must work together not only to deliver the service (blood test) but also to achieve a goal (accurate and timely test results). Lack of cooperation (an element of collaboration) by team members in any step in this service results in various negative outcomes, such as patient dissatisfaction, staff frustration, and delay or error in diagnosis or treatment.

More often than not, lack of collaboration stems from behavioral weaknesses, not deficiencies in technical knowledge and capacity. Behavioral weaknesses include poor communication, sabotage (conscious or unconscious) of existing processes, refusal to work with or participate in teams, gossip-mongering, apathy, procrastination and disregard for time frames, constant complaining and argumentativeness, rudeness, and resistance to constructive feedback. While these weaknesses may be chalked up to human nature, particularly if they occur only occasionally, they are disruptive nonetheless and signal that a bigger problem is at play. In other words, when blood results get mixed up in the lab or are lost in transit, the reasons likely have less to do with the technical aspects of the job than with the behavioral inadequacies among the staff. The challenge for leaders and managers is to observe, identify, and amend behavioral weaknesses so that they do not impede true collaboration.

A self-aware, influential leader champions health care collaboration, whether in the context of everyday work or as an organizational strategy. Self-awareness, as discussed in part I, enables a leader to (1) understand and respond to her own and others' behavior-based needs and (2) create a work team composed of people with diverse behavioral styles (see chapter 3) and technical strengths. A collaboration can be formed by any individuals or groups, but it cannot be sustained long enough to yield desired results without the guidance of a self-aware leader. Self-awareness is also the basis for the conforming dimension of the C^4 model. This dimension assesses a leader's awareness of the behaviors and approaches that are either conducive or harmful to team functioning.

In this chapter, the three traits of collaboration are described: (1) effective communication, (2) cooperative attitude, and (3) integrated team. In addition, examples of successful collaborative initiatives are presented. The underlying message in this chapter is that a culture of collaboration trumps competition in the quest to achieve performance excellence, but collaboration is not possible among team members who have more technical prowess than behavioral competencies. If you want to improve organizational outcomes, you have to start paying attention to interactions within your team.

Collaboration as a Performance Improvement Strategy

Organizations that are entrenched in the dated command-and-control leadership paradigm and "we work alone" mentality struggle to compete against organizations that embrace a culture of collaboration in which the employees are engaged, the work and goals are interdependent, and the leaders are self-aware but other-centered and connected. Modern health care has evolved to become consumer oriented, global, and information driven. In this environment, and in light of more health care reforms on the way, the expectations are greater than ever before:

- Health care consumers look for clinical transparency from providers,[1] as evident in the growing number of Web sites that publish hospital and physician ratings and medical outcomes data.[2]
- Leaders, in their quest to sustain operations, are compelled to study and create strategies for alignments and partnerships with other institutions.[3]
- The demand for cost control is prevalent. A new cost-control model is emerging. Currently called *accountable care organization,* this structure calls for physicians and hospitals to partner in coordinating and managing the care of a patient.[4]
- Employees in all industries want ethical, responsible leaders, a sentiment that represents a backlash against the many highly publicized cases of personal and professional indiscretions by people with power.

These expectations are just a few among the many, and all of them indicate that forging a collaboration is the most practical strategy for responding to the current and future realities in health care and for achieving performance excellence. This argument is echoed in The Governance Institute's publication

"Leadership in Healthcare Organizations: A Guide to Joint Commission Leadership Standards":[5]

> In a hospital, it is difficult—or, more accurately, impossible— for each leadership group, on its own, to achieve the goals of the hospital system: safe, high-quality care, accompanied by financial sustainability, community service, and ethical behavior. An all-wise governing body, an exceptionally competent chief executive and senior managers, and a medical staff composed of Nobel Prize-winning physicians cannot, each on their own, achieve safe, high-quality care, let alone all of these goals. An examination of the ingredients for safe care—the "first" obligation—elucidates the need for collaboration among these groups.

Furthermore, collaboration enriches the work lives of all the leaders, physicians and other caregivers, and staff associated with the organization. Collaboration emphasizes that everyone, no matter his position on the organizational chart, contributes to the goals of the enterprise. When someone asks you to get involved or to help, you feel needed, valued, and an integral part of a larger system. People who feel this way find their work meaningful, and as a result, they willingly contribute their time, talent, and energy and are motivated to perform at high levels. At the least, these people become advocates or supporters of the initiative. In this way, collaboration engages employees and encourages them to mind and/or improve their behavior.

The Three Traits of Collaboration

All three collaboration traits—effective communication, cooperative attitude, and integrated team—are based on the principles of human factors psychology, the study of human behavioral and thinking patterns and their influence on creating a better workplace, product, system, and so on. The task of forming and sustaining collaboration, then, is informed by human factors psychology as much as it, in turn, informs product design and manufacturing, for example. In other words, human factors psychology explains how people work, how they relate to each other and their environment, and why they work together.

Effective Communication

"What we've got here is a failure to communicate," says the captain in the movie *Cool Hand Luke*. This quotation articulates the communication challenges endemic in health care. The Joint Commission's 2010 National Patient Safety Goals for hospitals include "improve the effectiveness of communication among caregivers," indicating that sharing and coordinating critical information continue to be areas for improvement for many accredited institutions.

At a minimum, communication is the transmission of information, news, ideas, thoughts, and opinions between two or more parties. The means (verbal or in writing—on paper and electronically), modes (private or public, one-on-one or mass distribution), and style (formal or informal) of communication vary, depending on the purpose, urgency, and goal of the information. For example, if a leader wants to issue a general recognition note to all employees, he may opt to post his conversational and heartfelt message on the institution's intranet, tack it on bulletin boards, publish it in internal publications, or mention it when he meets employees face-to-face. He will not use the same tactics when he discusses a merger or an acquisition.

Much of the communication in health care delivery and management entails an exchange, wherein all the parties involved must act as both giver and recipient of information. This exchange ensures that the information is received and the recipient has an opportunity to express agreement, disagreement, confusion, understanding, need for clarification, or any other response. Ineffective communication results when a breakdown in this exchange occurs, and this breakdown can be exacerbated when electronic means are employed. Electronic devices crash, lose connectivity, become suddenly inoperable, and do not register human nuances. For example, a recent study by the Center for Studying Health System Change found that "reliance on EMRs [electronic medical records] could result in poorer communications with other providers in inpatient or clinical environments. While the use of other communication tools with EMRs—such as e mail and instant messaging—can sometimes help clinicians, they can also hinder care when a time lag occurs between responses."[6] (Although body language is a type of communication and cues us to a person's behavioral and mental patterns, to keep the discussion simple, it is not discussed here.)

Causes of ineffective communication are a mixture of both organizational and human factors. Time pressures, work stress, a multilayered corporate structure, language incompatibilities, and information overload are cited as some of the organization-related causes.[7] The human factors are mental, behavioral, and emotional weaknesses, such as the following:

- Poor listening skills
- Lack of focus or mental disorganization
- Impatience and arrogance
- Tendency to assume instead of double-check
- Uncontrolled emotional attachment or response to the information
- Disinterest in the information or the task
- Refusal to clarify and follow up
- Fatigue or burnout

People who display these and similar interpersonal inadequacies put themselves, their communication partners, and those affected by the information in a dangerous position. They send/receive only partial and possibly incorrect information, and consequently they create time-consuming double work, confusion, frustration, and conflict. In this case, communication will not improve if behaviors and mind-set do not improve.

Impact of Behavioral Style on Communication

Communication starts and stops all collaborations. We cannot begin to collaborate if we do not sit down for a discussion first, and we cannot continue our collaboration if we do not regularly communicate with our partners. Thus, effective communication is a critical component, especially for a team composed of people with diverse behavioral styles.

As discussed in chapter 3, our behavioral style (not to be confused with personality) is how we present ourselves to those around us. We show our style by the way we interact with others, communicate, manage ourselves, receive and process information, and respond to situations. We could be "analytical," "driver," "amiable," or "expressive." (See chapter 3 for the definitions of and variations on these terms.)

Different behavioral styles are necessary (and likely inevitable) in collaboration because the team faces many issues that demand multiple, varied approaches. The challenge for the collaboration team is to learn each member's behavioral style so that all communications take advantage of the strengths of each style and yield productive or desired results.

Figure 4-1 suggests approaches you can take to improve your communication in a collaboration.

Figure 4-1.   Try This: Five Don'ts of Collaborative Communication

---

These approaches work for both verbal and nonverbal exchanges with your team.

1. *Don't condescend.* Condescension is a nuanced practice; sometimes, it is hard to tell if we or others are involved in a condescending exchange. Generally, a statement that makes you seem superior to others and makes others feel inferior to you (and vice versa) is condescending. For example, "Let me put it in words you can understand" is condescending, and so is "I will repeat the information as many times as you need." Terms of endearment (e.g., dear, buddy, sweetheart, kid), no matter their intent, should also not be used in a professional setting. The key is to regard your collaboration partners as equals—people who have as much to offer as you do, regardless of titles and ranks.

(Continued on next page)

Figure 4-1.   (Continued)

2. *Don't speak before you listen.* No one seems to be patient anymore in our 24/7 world of information, where news, data, opinions, and recommendations are within reach on the Internet and through other electronic media. This constant accessibility has made us anxious to get to the "good part." In the process, when we interact with others, we interrupt, we hear instead of listen, we become defensive, and we think of a quick response instead of focusing on what is being said. Listen with all your senses: Pay attention to words, body language, tone, surrounding, and intent. Be aware of your own as well. Wait to speak; view the process of conversation as a capital investment— you would not sign off on the purchase of an expensive piece of equipment while in the middle of a cost analysis, so why would you respond before the other person can fully express the message?

3. *Don't be vague.* Be clear about your goals and expectations, and encourage others to articulate their wants and needs. This simple practice prevents you and your team from making assumptions, doing extra work, and accomplishing the wrong tasks or meeting the wrong targets. Follow up, clarify, repeat yourself, use a checklist, or write an outline, as necessary. The point of being clear is twofold: (1) to give collaboration partners a chance to disagree, ask questions, and offer compromises and (2) to ensure that all collaboration partners are headed toward the same direction.

4. *Don't withhold relevant information.* Provide needed resources to your team, including information that enables the team to do its job fully and well. Insight, lessons, and advice from experience are just as informative as facts and data. Share background, forecasts, current trends, and study findings as well as negative and positive intelligence. Urge every team member to do the same, and help each other cultivate and maintain a trust culture in which the information shared will not be used for sabotage or damage.

5. *Don't ignore conflict.* Even the most benign interactions can cause conflict. Consider this brief instruction: "Please hand in your report next week." The lack of specifics in this note can infuriate a busy team member, making her feel defensive, for starters. Despite our general aversion to conflict, we have to face it. Pretending it does not exist will only enlarge it and ruin the goodwill we have built with our collaboration partners. Listening, being objective, admitting to your mistakes and role in the problem, learning others' behavioral styles, keeping the situation fact based instead of emotion driven, and offering practical solutions are some ways to resolve and manage conflict.

Collaboration Tools and Examples

High-reliability organizations (HROs) are institutions or systems that "operate under very trying conditions all the time and yet manage to have fewer than their fair share of accidents."[8] Air traffic control systems, nuclear power plants, and airlines are examples of HROs. Five principles underlie the practices of HROs:[9]

1. Mindfulness
2. Reluctance to simplify interpretations
3. Sensitivity to operations
4. Commitment to resilience
5. Deference to expertise

These principles enable HROs to minimize their failure rates and consistently provide safe service.

High-reliability organizations have a lot to teach health care delivery, a theory that the Agency for Healthcare Research and Quality (AHRQ) sought to prove in 2005 when it formed a collaborative project to study how HRO principles can be/have been applied to hospital operations and what improvements can be/have been achieved. This collaboration included industry experts, HRO consultants, and leaders of both high-performing organizations and those still trying to improve their safety and quality. The lessons learned from this exercise are detailed in the document "Becoming a High Reliability Organization." It can be found online at www.ahrq.gov/qual/hroadvice/index.html.

Following are tools for and examples of leveraging the three elements of collaboration (communication, cooperation, and teamwork) to improve quality and safety in HROs. Note that these examples emphasize the human factors.

Crew Resource Management
Crew resource management (CRM) is a training program focused on improving decision making, communication, and teamwork in HROs. First used in a NASA workshop in 1979, CRM was developed following NASA's research finding that failures in human interaction are a major

contributor to deadly plane crashes and accidents. The premise of CRM is simple: "[use] all available sources—information, equipment, and people—to achieve safe and efficient flight operations."[10] Safety and efficiency increase when communication, cooperation, and teamwork take place among crew members and other personnel (e.g., air traffic controllers) who have disparate knowledge, skills, and responsibilities.

Crew resource management teaches skills that are especially germane to error-prone environments such as health care. It emphasizes clear communication, education, briefing and debriefing, conflict resolution, standardized practices, and error reporting.[11] Application of CRM in health care is not a new idea. It has been used in stressful patient care areas such as the intensive care unit, operating room, emergency department, and anesthesiology. Its use in health care has garnered support from influential bodies such as AHRQ, The Joint Commission, and the Institute for Healthcare Improvement.[12] In addition, a recent study found that CRM in health care "can influence personal behaviors and empowerment," although its "effects may take years to be ingrained into the culture."[13]

Safe Surgery 2015
Safe Surgery 2015 is a South Carolina program that calls on acute care providers statewide to adopt and implement the Safe Surgery Saves Lives Checklist, a guideline created by the World Health Organization to protect the health and lives of surgical patients around the world. This project is a collaboration in several ways. It is a joint endeavor among Every Patient Counts; the South Carolina Hospital Association; PHT Services Ltd.; and as of December 16, 2010, Dr. Atul Gawande, director of the World Health Organization's Global Challenge for Safer Surgery Care initiative. Its multiphase rollout is partnership oriented as well, relying on the full cooperation of hospital leadership, nurses, physicians, and other clinicians and personnel. In addition, Safe Surgery 2015 offers free CRM training to

surgical teams. The training sessions are taught by CRM specialists and incorporate open communication techniques, basic team formation, and behavioral impact on performance and patient safety.[14]

TeamSTEPPS

TeamSTEPPS® (Team Strategies and Tools to Enhance Performance and Patient Safety) is a collaborative initiative of the U.S. Department of Defense and AHRQ. Designed for health care professionals, TeamSTEPPS is an evidence-based, three-phase education and training program for teams. The approach, which is used in all military hospitals and other civilian systems, addresses team-related issues such as using and sharing information, managing conflict, establishing clear team roles and responsibilities, and eliminating barriers to excellent performance.[15] In addition, it provides assessment instruments, an SBAR (situation, background, assessment, recommendation) communication tool, and various other performance and handoff tools.[16]

The real value of TeamSTEPPS is that it provides guidance on sustaining the lessons learned. Nothing is more frustrating for leaders than the fact that after a development training, no change in behavior and practice can be seen from those who participated, rendering the educational investment useless. With TeamSTEPPS, a change team is formed to manage the training and implementation, increasing the likelihood that the training will be applied to everyday practice and spread across the organization. A study of the effectiveness of TeamSTEPPS in a labor and delivery unit of a military hospital found that it "improved time from decision to performance of cesarean section." This same study stated that "evaluations of the program in other settings have demonstrated its effectiveness, including reductions in medical errors, adverse events, length of stay, and employee turnover; better adherence to evidence-based practices; and enhanced provider satisfaction."[17]

Cooperative Attitude

Cooperation is the act of participating, contributing, or helping to advance or accomplish a goal. It is similar to collaboration in that cooperation requires the input of many people. But it is different in that those involved in cooperation do not necessarily have to be members of the collaboration, and as such these individuals or groups can have their own agendas but still contribute to the work of the collaboration.[18] For example, a collaboration between hospital executives and physicians benefits from the cooperation of nurses, other caregivers, and support staff. Collaboration cannot occur without cooperation, but cooperation can occur without formal collaboration.

Cooperative attitude is a mental model. It influences a person's desire and willingness to cooperate and produces an emotional response. For example, if an organization's vice president is convinced that cooperation creates more work but yields no advantage for himself and his department, he will not volunteer his skills and knowledge to the effort; if required to cooperate, he will perform halfheartedly, constantly question the necessity of the process, and harbor resentment. This behavior, in turn, poisons his staff and anyone with whom he has contact. Conversely, an executive with a positive attitude about cooperation will do what she can to help and will feel honored that she is a contributor. Her attitude then inspires and encourages her staff and associates to change their cooperation mind-set. Because a cooperative attitude is critical to true collaboration, leaders must work to change their own mental model and guide their followers to do the same.

A cooperative attitude inhibits competition. While competition between clinical teams is healthy in that it brings out personal and team bests, energy, and commitment to the work, it can quickly lead to dysfunctional behavior. Competition can turn some people into fanatics—so single-minded in their pursuit that they become blind to the consequences of their actions. They want to win at all costs, so they employ unfair practices, manipulate (and thus alienate) those around them, and ignore rules. In addition, "unhealthy competition can impact workers in ways a boss might not see coming. An obvious, though unwelcome, possibility is physical harm between co-workers."[19] Certainly, unhealthy competitive behavior has no place in a collaborative culture. Those who cooperate gain greater rewards than those who compete.

Integrated Team

An integrated team is a group composed of people with different areas of expertise and knowledge. Members of this team function in harmony, contributing their respective minds and talents toward the completion of a task or the realization of a goal. This team follows the systems model, whereby the work is interconnected and the workers are interdependent, so failure in one component can have disastrous effects on the rest of the system.

The Leadership Excellence Network, a collaboration between the National Center for Healthcare Leadership and General Electric, demonstrates the superiority of team decision making.[20] Early results show improvements in organizational climate, better understanding of organizational goals and expectations, greater individual and leader accountability, lower turnover, and higher retention of leader candidates. There is a caveat, however: While an integrated team is most optimal during an organizational crisis, it is usually at this time that conflict among members can occur. These conflicts are brought on by various factors, including, and most significantly, behavioral disconnect.

As stated earlier, anyone can put together an integrated team. But only an influential leader can create and sustain a highly functional integrated team. Sustaining such a team requires the leader to provide guidance and needed resources and then stay out of the way. Influential leaders know that micromanagement has no place in this equation, so they form a team whose members have behavioral competencies, including interpersonal skills that enhance the team members' financial, operational, clinical, and human resources knowledge and abilities. If members cannot get through to other people, their technical expertise will not advance the goals of the team. In the health care workplace, excellent outcomes are the product primarily of good people; the good process is a secondary factor in that success.

My consulting experience has taught me that in virtually every organization one person is universally regarded as detrimental to the mission, vision, values, and strategies of the enterprise. This is a person who comes to work every day intent on making the lives of everyone else a nightmare. This is a person whom others would like to fire had they the authority to do so. No organization needs a team member like this. The organization cannot become what its people are not; if employees are mediocre, the organization is equally mediocre. If an employee exhibits toxic behavior, the organization will also exhibit toxic behavior. No aspect of this scenario can be good for patient care.

Ultimately, creating *and* sustaining a highly functional integrated team necessitate developing strong relationships. Remember that we never get the relationships we wish for, but we do get the relationships we work for. And working for an effective team involves doing the following:

- Asking more than telling
- Expressing thanks and appreciation in both formal and informal ways
- Including the group in brainstorming and problem-solving processes
- Being approachable
- Rewarding cooperative and interdependent behavior, not "rock star" performance
- Hiring people who value and understand shared responsibility and accountability
- Staying committed to collaboration, not competition and conflict

Building a Culture of Collaboration

Installing a culture of collaboration (for the entire organization or a specific department) in which open communication, cooperative attitude, and integrated teams prevail does not happen easily or quickly. It is an intentional, purposeful undertaking that develops over many years and involves many players. The payoff, however, is immeasurable, as evidenced by the success at Advocate South Suburban Hospital in Hazel Crest, Illinois. Chief executive officer Dr. Ann Errichetti and her staff transformed South Suburban's culture into a collaborative environment in which open communication, patient-focused attitude, and integrated team are central. This change has yielded dramatic results in the hospital's emergency department, including decreases in waiting times, length of stay, and percentage of patients who leave without being seen. It has also improved staff morale, reduced staff turnover, and created a cost savings of more than $500,000.[21]

Lessons in Collaboration and Excellence
from the Mayo Clinic

The Mayo Clinic has been a leader in health care since the turn of the twentieth century. Its success in various areas of care delivery has been an inspiration to many organizations. Following is a brief description of Mayo's excellent collaborative approach.

- *Unhurried patient interaction.* Health care professionals at Mayo take time to listen to patient concerns, enabling them to better understand the root causes, risk factors, and consequences of ailments. This approach is not typical practice in the industry. If you have ever reviewed patient satisfaction surveys, you found that patients and/or their families consistently complain about how little time they spend with health care providers, giving them no time to discuss their conditions or ask about treatment options.

- *Team approach to medicine.* One hundred years ago, Dr. Will Mayo argued that "individualism can no longer exist" in medicine.[22] Today, the Mayo Clinic continues to support this idea. The organization makes it easy for doctors to work together by providing the best personnel, facilities, and technology available. Every patient is placed under the care of a coordinating physician, and that physician assembles a team to evaluate the patient's condition. This team, including the physician, is in constant contact and together discusses the diagnosis and comes up with treatment options. The team is also available to meet with the patient to answer questions, alleviate concerns, and explain procedures and next steps.

- *Technological advances.* Mayo's Media Support Services Division, a department that implemented the first medical photograph in 1905, supports the technological needs of the collaborative culture.[23] The department provides bandwidth support and other electronic communication tools.

- *Influential leadership.* The collaborative culture at Mayo discourages individual arrogance, which often taints otherwise competent health care professionals. The Mayo environment fosters collective ownership of decision making and outcomes. When mistakes arise, no finger pointing or blame shifting occurs, because accepting responsibility is a cultural value.

Source: Evan Rosen, *The Culture of Collaboration* (San Francisco: Red Ape Publishing, 2007).

Transforming a culture from independent and competitive to interdependent and collaborative is not uncomplicated. Following are just some of the barriers to this culture change:

- *Behavioral weaknesses.* According to research, high-performing health care professionals tend to share some performance strengths and weaknesses. The strengths include working memory, organizational ability, and planning/prioritizing. The weaknesses include stress tolerance, emotional control, and sustained attention.[24] Note that the strengths are technical oriented, while the weaknesses are behavior based. This finding supports the argument made earlier in the chapter that most of the time, behavioral weakness, not technical deficiency, is the main reason lack of collaboration, conflict, or failure occurs in a system.

A leader who continues to hone her technical strengths but ignores the effects of her behavioral weaknesses cannot be expected (or will find it difficult) to create, let alone sustain, a culture of collaboration. This is a probable reason for the overall leveling off of performance in health care despite the development and implementation of quality improvement approaches, enhanced technology, and standardized processes. In fact, Joint Commission data show an increase in sentinel events in five of ten areas from 2008 to 2009.[25]

• *Slow adoption of change.* The problem with exporting a collaborative culture, like that at the Mayo Clinic, to current operations is similar to the problem faced when introducing a best practice or new approach: The process is slow. Hospitals greatly benefit from the services and expertise of physicians, boards, employees, administrators, and other partners, but these groups have agendas that can slow down, clash with, or stop the adoption of change. This situation is compounded by human factors, such as people's natural anxiety about change. Even when provided evidenced-based data, we are slow adopters. In fact, the British Navy took 127 years to codify the use of citrus fruits to prevent scurvy on board its ships; this is 127 years *after* science proved that a daily fruit ration is effective in warding off scurvy.[26]

- *Top-down decision-making structure.* Organizational performance is a leader's responsibility. Unfortunately, many leaders tend to take this duty literally, acting as the first and final decision maker on all financial and operational matters. On his own, the leader assesses problems, comes up with a plan of action, announces his decision to senior management, and orders the plan to be rolled out immediately. He does not consult with his leadership team, and he does not expect or welcome resistance or questions. "Solutions" developed independently create more problems because they lack the perspective of the people who are directly affected by the implementation. Many process improvements fail for this very reason. This top-down environment breeds cynicism, dissatisfaction, infighting, and other negative behaviors and emotions.

- *Lack of shared conviction.* Leaders must clearly communicate the "why" of change—the conviction behind any initiative. Followers are more likely to adopt change when they fully understand what they are getting into. They need to know why the change is important and how the change will help and hinder their work and environment. They need motivation and inspiration, and they will get neither if leaders are not forthcoming with information or are focused on implementation (the "how" of change) rather than education. The approaches of influential leaders are directly opposite those of command-and-control leaders. Influential leaders invest ample time to communicate the why. They volunteer relevant information, tell inspiring success stories, share both advantages and disadvantages of the change, and encourage staff involvement in the process.

Every influential leader has experienced some or all of these barriers. However, these leaders have viewed them as opportunities rather than as impediments. By looking at these problems as an open door to improvement or as a way out of the status quo, influential leaders welcome with open arms the challenge of transforming or creating a new culture. They start the change process with themselves, and then they move on to their teams and on to the rest of the organization.

Creating a culture of collaboration means eliminating and mitigating behavioral weaknesses that disrupt communication, foster uncooperative attitudes, erode trust, and breed dysfunctional teams. Perhaps the most important part of this culture change process is the influential leader's ability to guide others to conform to the desired mind-set and behavior that are conducive to collaboration.

Three Steps for Sustaining Collaboration

1. *Establish behavior-based expectations.* These expectations include the behaviors and values you want the team to display as they perform their duties and interact with each other and the rest of the organization. Documents that may guide you in establishing these expectations are the mission, vision, and values statements of the organization. Behavior-based expectations guide team members in various ways—from how to treat each other on a daily basis to how to handle conflict to what accountability entails. This document must be specific and clear so that it becomes a useful tool for both employees and leaders. I have had an opportunity to help create such a standard, called ICARE, which stands for Integrity, Compassion, Accountability, Respect, Excellence. The ICARE standard is widely used and has helped encourage cooperative attitudes and open communication. See chapter 5 for strategies to create accountability behavior standards.

2. *Hold yourself accountable.* The leader's character and technical competence alone do not inspire people to become better communicators, to cooperate willingly, and to trust others. What followers need is for you to

take responsibility for your decisions, actions, direc-
tives, and strategies. If you do not do the right thing in
the right way and for the right reasons, then you must
own up to your mistakes. Do not make excuses, blame
someone else for your shortcomings, or feel victimized
by the system. If you do, you are not modeling accountable behaviors and cannot expect your followers to be
accountable themselves. Fix the problem immediately,
and apologize—these actions go a long way toward
regaining your team's trust.

3. *Listen, and encourage two-way communication.* Stephen
Covey may have said it best in his book *The 7 Habits of
Highly Effective People*: "seek to understand before we
demand to be understood."[27] Communication is not just
about conveying information; it is also about exchanging ideas. Active listening is a significant part of this
exchange. Leaders who talk but do not listen learn nothing about themselves and about others, and collaboration
cannot develop from this approach.

Even hard-charging leaders are aware of the value of
two-way communication.

The Conforming Dimension of the C⁴ Model

Poor interpersonal behaviors promote dysfunctional relationships
that ultimately result in poor organizational outcomes. Collaboration is lost in this equation, if it even took root to begin with.

The conforming dimension of the C^4 model allows us to
examine, and thus guide, behaviors in the context of team functioning and performance. Conforming is related to the first three
dimensions of the C^4 model in that it relies on self-awareness
skills and knowledge. The focus of conforming, however, is
external instead of internal. Its purpose is to identify behaviors
that either contribute to or take away from the team's objectives
and the overall collaborative culture. In this process of examination, you will be able to determine how good behaviors can be

encouraged (i.e., rewarded, celebrated) and how poor behaviors can be improved. Then you can create behavior based expectations that drive performance toward your desired outcomes.

When people's behavioral weaknesses are explained to them in terms of their actual negative impact, they pay closer attention to their behaviors in the future. For example, if you tell a perfectionist vice president of clinical services that her behavior is directly contributing to the staff attrition in her department, she will get defensive at first but will ask you for specific information soon after. Similarly, when nurses and physicians are told that their impatient and haughty bedside manner is causing inpatients to lie about symptoms or refuse further treatment, these clinicians will alter their approach at their next visit.

While an organization's culture can take years to change, individual behavior can be expected to change as soon as possible, depending on the urgency of the situation. Thus, assessing the conforming dimension is important—the quicker you identify what works and what does not work about your team or teams, the quicker you can design an improvement plan for the individuals and the quicker you can apply these improvements to the rest of the organization.

When you invest in a culture of collaboration, you enable employees to engage in their work and produce exceptional results. But first, you must start to convince these employees to conform.

Conclusion

Poor behavior will never drive performance excellence and will always harm patients, because it cannot bring people together to create anything of value. Without collaboration, competition and conflict reign—two conditions in which medical errors are highly likely, staff morale and motivation are low, performance is inconsistent and unreliable, communication and cooperation are nonexistent, and everyone has a secret agenda.

Key Takeaways

- Collaboration is a partnership between people and/or groups intended to generate a product or achieve a singular objective that is mutually beneficial to all parties involved.

- Lack of collaboration stems from behavioral weaknesses, not deficiencies in technical knowledge and capacity.

- A collaboration can be formed by anybody, but it cannot be sustained long enough to yield desired results without the guidance of a self-aware leader.

- The three traits of collaboration are described: (1) effective communication, (2) cooperative attitude, and (3) integrated team.

- A culture of collaboration trumps competition in the quest to achieve performance excellence, but collaboration is not possible among team members who have more technical prowess than behavioral competencies.

- Collaboration enriches the work lives of people, making them feel that their work is meaningful. As a result, they willingly contribute their time, talent, and energy and are motivated to perform at high levels.

- Much of the communication that takes place in health care delivery and management entails an exchange wherein all the parties involved must act as both giver and recipient of information. Ineffective communication results when a breakdown in this exchange occurs.

- Differing behavioral styles is necessary (and likely inevitable) in collaboration because the team faces many issues that demand multiple, varied approaches.

- Cooperation is the act of participating, contributing, or helping to advance or accomplish a goal. It is different from collaboration in that those involved in cooperation do not necessarily have to be members of the collaboration.

- Collaboration cannot occur without cooperation, but cooperation can occur without formal collaboration.

- A cooperative attitude inhibits competition. While competition between clinical teams is healthy in that it brings out personal and team bests, energy, and commitment to the work, it can quickly lead to dysfunctional behavior.

- An integrated team is a group composed of people with different areas of expertise and knowledge.

- The organization cannot become what its people are not; if employees are mediocre, the organization is equally mediocre.

- Installing a culture of collaboration does not happen easily or quickly. It is an intentional, purposeful undertaking that develops over many years and involves many players. The payoff, however, is immeasurable.

- The most important part of this culture change process is the influential leader's ability to guide others to conform to the desired mind-set and behavior that are conducive to collaboration.

- The conforming dimension of the C^4 model guides us in examining, and thus understanding, behaviors in the context of team functioning and performance. The purpose of conforming is to identify behaviors that either contribute to or take away from the team's objectives and the overall collaborative culture.

- While an organization's culture can take years to change, individual behavior can be expected to change as soon as possible, depending on the urgency of the situation.

- When you invest in a culture of collaboration, you enable employees to engage in their work and produce exceptional results. But first, you must start to convince these employees to conform.

Applying the C⁴ Model:
Collaboration and Conforming

The following questions are intended to initiate self-examination of the collaborative components—communication, cooperation, and integrated team—in your organization and group. Take the time to think about these questions, and be honest with yourself.

- Articulate your thoughts on collaboration. How is it practiced, encouraged, or pursued in your organization? What collaborations have you forged within and outside of the organization? What negative and positive outcomes has collaboration produced? Do you have a collaborative culture? How did it come about, and how are you trying to sustain it?

- Describe the team's communication approach. How does it help or hinder the spread or sharing of information? What tools and resources are available to the team to facilitate communication among members and between members and other cooperative partners?

- Are you aware of every team member's behavioral style or preference? How do these styles complement or conflict with each other? What effects do these differing styles have on the team's interaction? Are these styles conducive to collaboration? If so, how? If not, what are you doing to remedy the situation?

- What is the level of integration or interdependency in your organization? If the organization still follows the individualist approach, what advantages and disadvantages has it brought your team? Is your team knowledgeable about or at least familiar with the systems approach? If so, how is the systems approach applied day to day?

- What kinds of conflict do you/your team face every day? List the top three conflicts that recur. What percentage of these conflicts is associated with behavioral weaknesses, and what percentage is associated with technical deficiencies? What tactics are usually employed to solve these conflicts?

- What is the current level of cooperation among and between teams, units, and departments? If this level is low, what do you think contributes to this deficiency, and what are the consequences?

- What are the decision-making, problem-solving, and brainstorming processes in your organization? How are all members of the team involved? If involvement is low, how well are decisions supported and implemented? If involvement is high, what kind of accountability is required of everyone?

- Consider your team's successes and failures. What have been the factors (including behavioral and technical) that contributed to the success and failure? Have you and your team sat down to analyze and discuss these factors for the purpose of either replicating or eliminating them?

- Do your teams participate in healthy competition, and with whom and over what? What are the advantages and disadvantages of this practice? Has this practice ever devolved into unhealthy competition? If so, recall the events, including why the unhealthy competition occurred and how it was resolved.

References

1. Accenture, "The American Public on Health Care: The Missing Perspective," 2010 [http://www.accenture.com/Global/Services/By_Industry/Health_and_Life_Sciences/Government_Health/R_and_I/AmericanHealthCareMissPer.htm]. Accessed September 3, 2010.
2. T. Krohn, "Hospital Outcomes Tracked on Web. Federal Report Now Online," *The Free Press* (Mankato, MN), 2010 [http://mankato freepress.com/local/x993511939/Hospital-outcomes-tracked-on-Web]. Accessed September 3, 2010.

3. E. O'Neil, "Competencies for a Reformed Health Care Environment," July 2010 [http://futurehealth.ucsf.edu/Public/Publications-and-Resources/Content.aspx?topic=Competencies_for_a_Reformed_Health_Care_Environment]. Accessed September 3, 2010.

4. E. Gardner, "Loads of Potential," *Modern Healthcare*, 2010 [http://www.modernhealthcare.com/article/20100726/MAGAZINE/100729966]. Accessed September 3, 2010.

5. P.M. Schyve, "Leadership in Healthcare Organizations: A Guide to Joint Commission Leadership Standards," Governance Institute white paper, November 2009 [http://www.jointcommission.org/assets/1/18/WP_Leadership_Standards.pdf]. Accessed September 3, 2010.

6. J. Simmons, "Can EMRs Lead to a Failure to Communicate?" *HealthLeaders Media*, 2010 [http://www.healthleadersmedia.com/content/QUA-250289/Can-EMRs-Lead-to-a-Failure-to-Communicate]. Accessed September 3, 2010.

7. ManagementStudyGuide.com, "Communication Barriers—Reasons for Communication Breakdown" [http://www.managementstudyguide.com/communication_barriers.htm]. Accessed September 3, 2010.

8. K.E. Wieck and K.M. Sutcliffe, *Managing the Unexpected: Assuring High Performance in an Age of Complexity* (San Francisco: Jossey-Bass, 2001).

9. Ibid.

10. L. Pizzi, N.I. Goldfarb, and D.B. Nash, 2001. "Crew Resource Management and Its Applications in Medicine," AHRQ Evidence Reports, 2001 [http://www.ncbi.nlm.nih.gov/bookshelf/br.fcgi?book=erta43&part=A64100]. Accessed September 3, 2010.

11. C. Konschak and L. Jarrell, "Flying Lessons: Crew Resource Management in Healthcare," 2010 [http://www.divurgent.com/images/CRMWHITEPAPER.PDF]. Accessed September 3, 2010.

12. Ibid.

13. H. Sax, P. Browne, R.J. Mayewski, R.J. Panzer, K.C. Hittner, R.L. Burke, and S. Coletta, "Can Aviation-Based Team Training Elicit Sustainable Behavioral Change?" *Archives of Surgery* 144, no. 12 (2009): 1133–1137.

14. Every Patient Counts, "Operation: Safe Surgery" [http://www.everypatient.net/operation-safe-surgery]. Accessed September 3, 2010.

15. Agency for Healthcare Research and Quality (AHRQ), "About TeamSTEPPS" [http://teamstepps.ahrq.gov/about-2cl_3.htm]. Accessed September 3, 2010.

16. Ibid.

17. AHRQ Health Care Innovations Exchange, "Teamwork Enhancement Program Improves Obstetric Care in a Military Hospital," November 2008 [http://www.innovations.ahrq.gov/content.aspx?id= 1702#?]. Accessed September 3, 2010.

18. G. Cuppan, "Just What Do We Mean by Collaborative vs. Cooperative?" 2009 [http://brain.brainery.net/mcblog/?p=255]. Accessed September 3, 2010.

19. A. Balderrama, "When Does Competition with a Co-worker Go Too Far?" February 2009 [http://www.careerbuilder.com/Article/CB-1122-The-Workplace-When-Does-Competition-With-a-Co-worker-Go-Too-Far/]. Accessed September 3, 2010.

20. *Chief Learning Officer*, "Executive Briefings," 2009 [http://www.clomedia.com/industry_news/2009/December/5095/index.php]. Accessed December 15, 2009.

21. J. Towne, "Engaging Employees," *Hospitals & Health Networks*, February 2009 [http://www.hhnmag.com/hhnmag_app/jsp/articledisplay.jsp?dcrpath=HHNMAG/Article/data/02FEB2009/090210HHN_Online_Towne&domain=HHNMAG]. Accessed December 9, 2010.

22. E. Rosen, *The Culture of Collaboration* (San Francisco: Red Ape Publishing, 2007, 24).

23. Ibid.

24. *Chief Learning Officer*, "Executive Briefings."

25. K. Terry, "Do You Hold Staff Accountable for Safety?" *Hospitals & Health Networks*, February 2010 [http://www.hhnmag.com/hhnmag_app/jsp/articledisplay.jsp?dcrpath=HHNMAG/Article/data/02FEB2010/1002HHN_FEA_patientsafety&domain=HHNMAG]. Accessed February 11, 2010.

26. *Nutrition Health Review*, "A Short History of Scurvy," spring 1992 [http://findarticles.com/p/articles/mi_m0876/is_n62/ai_12296592]. Accessed December 9, 2010.

27. S. Covey, *The 7 Habits of Highly Effective People*, rev. ed. (New York: Free Press, 2004).

5

Trust:
The Heart of Collaboration

*Organizations typically spend considerable energy and effort
in team building initiatives, including workshops, retreats,
and adventure type experiences. While all of these have their
place, if organizations want to increase collaboration and
enhance teamwork, they need to start with trust.*
—Bruna Martinuzzi, leadership consultant and
emotional intelligence expert

Trust is a complex and far-reaching concept that pervades our personal and professional pursuits. We cannot bottle and sell it, and we cannot fully appreciate its enormous role in shaping constructs in society, including commerce, politics, and religion. Nonetheless, cultivating trust is an imperative, especially in organizational life. It increases the likelihood that people will engage and collaborate: They will communicate openly, adopt cooperative attitudes, and work in an integrated team with a shared responsibility for shared objectives. When trust is absent, damaged, or lost in the workplace, relationships are dysfunctional and work effectiveness and performance suffer.

This chapter explains the critical role that trust plays in all the tasks and duties of an influential leader, including building a collaborative culture. The concept of the emotional bank account as a source of trust is also discussed.

Trust in the Context of Teams

The word *trust* is derived from *trost*, a German term that suggests comfort. This is an appropriate association because when we trust someone, we are comforted by the belief that this person has our best interest at heart and thus will not endanger us or put us at risk. Because trust is a critical component in all human interactions, it has many types. Following are two that are encountered most often in a team setting:

1. *Generalized.* We trust on the basis of our mental model that people are generally honorable. Generalized trust is a leap of faith in that we choose to trust without evidence that our trust is deserved or without concrete assurance that whom we trust will deliver good results. As social and ethical theorist Russell Hardin puts it, "generalized trust must be a matter of relatively positive expectations of the trustworthiness, cooperativeness, and helpfulness of others."[1]

2. *Behavioral.* We bestow our trust on the basis of the person's good behavior. That is, if someone has exhibited reliability, honesty, competencies, compassion, or courage over time, that person earns our trust. *Earn* is the operative word here. Trust does not come automatically with positions of power. Even if it did, however (as in the case with generalized trust), trust cannot be sustained by virtue of rank alone. It must be supported by ongoing good behavior, which then validates our confidence.

This chapter focuses on the second type of trust—behavioral. Trust-earning behaviors include the following:

- Consistency in manner, words, and actions
- Accountability and transparency, including actively listening, sharing information, and taking responsibility instead of blaming
- Genuine or sincere interest in and concern for others
- Respectful and equal regard for and treatment of others, regardless of rank and position

- Focused attention
- Principled and evidence based decision making
- Dedication to fulfilling (not just making) promises
- Willingness to celebrate and reward good and exceptional work

These behaviors depict the self-aware traits of influential leaders. As masters of interpersonal relations, influential leaders know that their everyday words and actions can either strengthen or weaken trust. People can take only so much bad behavior before they lose their faith and start to feel disconnected from their leaders and the organization.

Trust Bank Account

Stephen Covey applies his emotional bank account framework (see the discussion in chapter 3) to trust.[2] In a team setting, trust is a currency exchanged between members. Dependable behavior is a "deposit," while self-centered and opportunistic conduct is a "withdrawal." Trust deposits and withdrawals are made throughout the time the team is together, allowing each member to either gain or lose support. Covey proposes the idea of a trust bank account to give team members a common language for understanding and managing their relationship.

The following principles further explain Covey's trust account framework. It emphasizes that no "one size fits all" approach exists to earning and sustaining trust, so each member of the team must be aware of the factors that either amass or deplete trust.

- *Each trust account is unique.* Personal accounts are separate from professional accounts, and each kind involves different players and thus carries varying significance. For example, the trust account someone holds with a spouse is not the same as the account shared with the chief operating officer of the organization.

- *All deposits and withdrawals are not created equal.* A deposit or withdrawal in one trust account may not count as a deposit or withdrawal in another, because each of our account partners has different expectations. For example, failing to deliver on a project commitment has a different withdrawal consequence than forgetting to send a birthday card. Complicating this lack of deposit and withdrawal equality in a global economy is the ethnic-background diversity of the workforce, providers, patient population, and other partners. In some cultures, for example, simple hand gestures (e.g., thumbs up, wave) have implications that are opposite from their meanings in the American culture.[3] As a result, if we are to use these seemingly banal gestures in our communication, they could be misconstrued as rude, causing an unforeseen withdrawal from the trust account. Similarly, a person's behavioral style could affect his or her ideas of trust deposits and withdrawals. A person with an expressive style, for instance, will consider a public acknowledgment of accomplishments as a deposit, while a person with an analytical style may view that act as a withdrawal.

- *Withdrawals are typically larger than deposits.* A single, severely poor behavior (withdrawal) can instantly empty out the trust account, regardless of how long and how much you have deposited. Once the account is wiped out, the only option available to you is to humbly apologize. The response to this apology will determine whether you can again build up your trust reserve.

- *The fastest way to save trust is to stop making withdrawals.* We all have bad days, and as a result we have occasional lapses in judgment. Some people, however, consistently choose to behave badly, inconsiderate of the trust-eroding effects of their conduct. Essentially, trust is withdrawn but seldom deposited, creating a negative balance. Such members have no place on any team, let alone a high-functioning one. An influential leader is well aware of the damage that these members cause and does not tolerate anyone's conscious decision to act poorly. Team members who withdraw from more than deposit to the team's trust account initially get help and guidance from the influential leader, but over time, if they do not (or refuse to) improve, they are dismissed quickly. These members are toxic to team functioning, organizational growth, and any collaborative initiatives.

If you find yourself withdrawing from more than depositing into your trust accounts, you can take the following actions in each withdrawal situation:

- Clarify why you behaved poorly.
- Apologize and seek forgiveness.
- Reflect on the poor behavior, and work hard to change your mental model relating to it.
- Allow the other person time to process your explanation and to make a decision about restoring his or her trust in you.
- Choose to behave better in the future.

Levels of Trust

A level of trust must exist among members of a team. It enables the team not only to perform its functions but also to rise above conflicts and crises. Ideally, trust should be at a high level, but at a minimum, it should be at an acceptable level, allowing the team to develop and execute plans. Absence of trust almost always brings about bad consequences. As indicated in a study by Deloitte titled "Trust in the Workplace: 2010 Ethics & Workplace Survey," both employees and executives who participated in the survey agreed that lack of trust hurts morale. In addition, executives responded that the presence of no trust damages productivity and profitability.[4] Simply stated, low or no trust puts the organization at a competitive and performance disadvantage.

Figure 5-1 is an instrument for assessing and reflecting on the trust levels in your team. This tool measures specific behaviors that enable trust.

Emotional Component

As mentioned, behavior stirs up emotions. Trust can be held hostage by a negative emotional reaction; conversely, it can be elevated by a positive emotional response.

For example, if you have all the other qualities of a trustworthy leader (e.g., operationally and financially competent, experienced, forward thinking, and high performing) but occasionally throw tantrums around the office or at meetings, you are in danger of losing your team's trust. Your team will see you as reliable only in terms of belittling them, not in terms of championing their efforts. The team emotions that arise from your poor behavior include fear, intimidation, anger, self-loathing, hatred, de-motivation, and resentment. These feelings are not favorable to cultivating trust, let alone building a collaborative culture.

The reverse of this situation is ideal. Your good behavior instills in others a feeling of harmony, goodwill, and respect. They are willing to listen to your ideas, and they want to execute your plans in the best way possible.

Exercise: Emotions-Based Trust

Let's give this idea a practical application to your daily work life. Complete the following exercise. Do not skip to the next item until you have completed the one before.

1. Pick a team member whom you work with regularly.
2. Take a sheet of paper and make two columns. On the right column, write down your positive emotions about this person. On the left column, write down your negative

Figure 5-1.   Try This: Assess the Trust Levels in Your Team

Rate each statement below using this key: "0" if the statement does not apply, "1" if you do not agree, "2" if you agree slightly, and "3" if you agree completely. Then tally the ratings and find the corresponding score at the end of this tool.

1. Every member of the team is accountable and takes responsibility for his or her actions, words, and responsibilities.   _____

2. Team communication is open, with information sharing, team problem solving and analysis, and honest discourse taking place without fear of retaliation.   _____

3. The team leader is not a micromanager and regularly shows confidence in and respect for the team.   _____

4. All team members are engaged in their tasks and are interested in participating.   _____

5. Side deals, if discovered, are not tolerated, and team-established rules are enforced.   _____

6. All team members, including the leader, do what they say they will do.   _____

7. The team leader provides the necessary resources (e.g., insight, information, time, staff, money, training) to enable the team to achieve its goals.   _____

8. All team members are regarded as contributors (not just as warm bodies) whose skills, knowledge, and abilities add value to the team.   _____

9. The team culture emphasizes interdependency, encouraging cooperation and collaboration among members.   _____

10. Attitudinal and behavioral conflicts are dealt with immediately.   _____

Ratings total: _____

Scoring key:

1–10:   No or low level of trust, minimal cooperation, and minimal collaboration

11–20: Acceptable level of trust, some cooperation, and some collaboration

21–30: High level of trust, high cooperation, and high collaboration

emotions about this person. Consider the following questions while you complete this exercise:

- What does it feel like to spend a full day with this person? If you did not have to work with this person, would you socialize with him or her outside of the organization?

- Is this person cooperative or a team player? Competent? Intelligent? Reliable? Resourceful?

- Do you trust this person's judgment, words, and deeds? Is he or she conscientious?

- Is this person approachable? Accessible? Concerned about others' problems? Willing to help? Forthcoming with relevant information?

- How is this person perceived by other team members?

- Will you vouch for this person's character and integrity? Will you support his or her initiatives as a result?

- Is this person a positive or negative presence on the team?

Remember to write down only emotional responses, not traits of the person you selected.

3. Compare the right column with the left column. Have you listed more emotions on the left side than on the right, or vice versa? Or are an even number of emotions listed on both columns?

The items listed on the left column represent the emotions that decrease trust, while the items on the right are emotions that increase trust. Team members (including leaders) whose behaviors consistently cause emotions that fall into the left column engender a low-trust culture. These members may be highly productive and may drive the team to high profitability, but hardly anyone wants to work with them or genuinely supports their initiatives. Trust in this situation is minimal (falling in the generalized trust category, perhaps)—enough that we are able to meet performance expectations, but not enough to catapult us to excellence.

This kind of operating system is not at all sustainable or acceptable. Worse, bad emotions stirred up by inappropriate behavior are contagious. It is easy to become the people you dislike if you are surrounded by them every day. Eventually, without intervention, you may begin to show dysfunctional behavior, which will then trickle down to others on your team or move outside your team. This is the dark side of influence.

Connection to the Brain

Neuroscientists have discovered that oxytocin, a hormone and neurotransmitter, increases a person's willingness to trust others. The findings indicate that when someone is in a safe, nurturing environment, his or her brain releases more oxytocin.[5] A nonthreatening relationship is necessary for trust to grow and to be perceived. Conversely, early experiences of stress, worry, fear, and doubt interfere with the development of a trusting disposition and decrease oxytocin levels. This research finding validates and reinforces the message in this chapter: Good behavior promotes feelings of trust.

The connection between how the brain works and how we develop trust may be the reason it takes so much effort to rebuild a relationship damaged by the loss of trust. Essentially, our brains must be rewired to enable us to replace bad memories with caring experiences. This rewiring must be a mutual effort between the people in the relationship, requiring an even give-and-take. That is, I will work hard to change my behavior and mind-set, and you must work just as hard to change your perception and not punish me for what I have done in the past. This may be the first step to repairing trust.

In the past several years alone, there has been no shortage in the United States of public apologies and reports about the breach of trust committed by both private citizens and public figures. The problem is nationwide, and it crosses all fields, from politics to business, religion to professional sports. That represents a lot of brains to rewire, a lot of relationships to revive, and a lot of mutual work to accomplish. The good news is that trust, this very important intangible of life, can be built where it does not exist, can be increased when it is scant, and can be regained when it is lost.

Trust and Collaboration

The fundamental purposes of building and sustaining trust are to accomplish tasks and achieve goals. This is true for any enterprise, whether for-profit or not-for-profit. In this way, trust is an operational and collaborative imperative. In health care organizations, lack of trust leads to below-average safety, quality, and patient and provider satisfaction.

Influential leaders are acutely aware that trust and collaboration are inseparable. Trust and collaboration share the same purpose, and without trust any collaboration becomes a farce. After all, people—not processes, policies, strategies, tools, or methods—make up the collaboration, and trust is critical in motivating these people to do the actual work.

Influential leaders also know that trust begins and ends with their own behavior. Technical mastery, intelligence, personal and professional drive, past accomplishments, and even vision are admirable and necessary leadership qualities, but they alone do not inspire long-term trust and collaboration. These qualities must be complemented by interpersonal and behavioral competencies. A leader's high degree of credibility is the sum of both behavioral and technical skills, and this credibility is what initiates trust. Consistent display of credibility is what sustains trust. Trust, in turn, leads followers to support the concept of collaboration at first and then, ultimately, to fully participate in or pursue collaborations.

As mentioned earlier, in the absence of credible leaders, people will still perform their tasks and abide by organizational rules. They only do so, however, because they want to keep their job, and they perform at the lowest acceptable level possible. Obviously, this response is a narrow perspective that produces superficial results. A collaboration that is built on trust has a deeper meaning and thus has long-lasting power. It energizes, engages, and awakens passion and commitment, even in health care, where many workers suffer from compassion fatigue—the stress, isolation, pain, and apathy felt by caregivers.

Influential leaders are not just passive recipients of trust; they are also proactive givers of trust. They view trust as a mutual practice: They work hard to earn and keep it, and they expect and demand others to do the same. By displaying trustworthy behavior every day, influential leaders serve as a model to their followers and other partners. For example, influential leaders spend time contemplating the qualities and qualifications of candidates for a senior leadership position. They do not hire quickly to expedite the recruitment and hiring processes, especially when the position has been open for a long time. Their goal is to find the most ideal match for the organization and its culture. This reflective practice accomplishes two goals: (1) It lessens the risk of hiring a selfish, uncooperative leader who could undermine the collective success of the leadership team, and (2) it sends the message to the entire organization that the influential leader is serious about building and strengthening trust.

I am familiar with a health care organization that had great potential for creating high levels of organizational performance excellence. Unfortunately, the one key ingredient for excellence, trust among the leadership team, was missing, which was reflected in the safety, quality, service, and financial performance indicators of the organization. The impact of the low level of trust rippled through the entire organization.

Cynicism about Interpersonal Skills

In my teaching and consulting work, I encounter many leaders who acknowledge the combined power of trust and collaboration.

However, this power is not leveraged within many leadership teams, which seems to indicate two factors at play:

1. Many leaders have not chosen the endless rewards of collaboration with trust over the good-enough status quo.
2. Many leaders consider the concept of improving interpersonal behavior to be "soft" science.

Viewing the interpersonal components (e.g., trust, values, collaboration, self-awareness, engagement) of leadership as "soft" and "nice but unnecessary" can severely affect the "hard" components (e.g., financial, technical).[6] In addition, this perspective is shortsighted in today's consumer-driven environment, where the expectations are increasingly focused on leadership accountability and transparency. Simply, health care consumers and the public at large want ethical and conscientious hospitals and providers, and these ethical organizations are not led by people who lack interpersonal skills and only care about making money. The hard truth is that health care leadership is and will always be about making a positive difference in people's lives. That focus is easy to lose in economically challenging times, as we all scramble to grow our revenues, but it must stay on our minds daily.

The first step in cultivating and sustaining trust, a huge driver of interpersonal skills, is to accept that trust does not operate well under the "fake it 'til you make it" mind-set. You cannot pretend to be trustworthy, at least not for a long period. Similarly, you cannot pretend that you trust others, as they, too, cannot fake trustworthiness. Behaviors, particularly during times of stress, will always reveal what you really think and feel.

Assessing the Conforming Dimension of the C⁴ Model

The first three components of the C^4 model—conviction, convincing, and compelling—assess the leader's level of self-awareness. The fourth component—conforming—determines the leader's understanding of collaborative behaviors. Conforming relies heavily on the principles of self-awareness: Without self-awareness, a leader has no foundation for developing, sustaining, and modeling trust.

The conforming dimension asks the leader to evaluate the levels of several factors that exist within the team. This examination guides the leader in creating a plan for improvement. Low levels of these factors, such as the following, indicate that trust is low and collaboration is superficial and fleeting:

- Commitment to the work and to each other
- Sharing of information
- Communication that is considerate of behavioral styles or preferences
- Honesty and integrity
- Empowerment and participation
- Fairness and consistency
- Mutual respect for dignity and for skills and abilities

Along with the conforming assessment, the team may conduct a behavioral-style profile exercise that involves the entire team. This exercise reveals each team member's communication preference and social style, creating a comprehensive picture of the person's behavior motivations. Style profiling is based on scientific theories, which helps eliminate the misconception that interpersonal skills programs and workshops are "soft." This exercise should be held in a safe, relaxed environment where people will not be judged or harassed for the negative traits and practices that they disclose or that come up. Often, this exercise is led by a behavioral-style expert, which increases the credibility of the results and decreases the possibility of confirmation bias.

For more assessment questions related to the conforming dimension, see the "Applying the C^4 Model" section at the end of the chapter.

Conclusion

Influential leadership is inextricably linked to the trust intangible. When a disparity or misalignment exists between the conviction and values we profess and the behavior we exhibit, we create confusion and distrust among our teams. Influential leaders are living, breathing embodiments of the organization's mission, vision, and values. As such, they are able to deposit regularly into their trust bank accounts, thus inspiring better behavior among their followers and motivating collaboration. Without trust there is no influence, and without influence there is no opportunity to reach peak performance. As leadership experts Warren Bennis and Burt Nanus write, "Trust is the emotional glue that binds followers and leaders together. The accumulation of trust is a measure of legitimacy of leadership. It cannot be mandated or purchased; it must be earned. Trust is the basic ingredient of all organizations, the lubrication that maintains organizations."[7]

Key Takeaways

- Cultivating trust is an imperative. It increases the likelihood that people will communicate openly, adopt cooperative attitudes, and work in an integrated team with a shared responsibility for shared objectives.
- When trust is absent, damaged, or lost in the workplace, relationships are dysfunctional and work effectiveness and performance suffer.
- Generalized trust is a leap of faith: We choose to trust without evidence that our trust is deserved or without concrete assurance that whom we trust will deliver good results.
- Behavioral trust is earned on the basis of reliability, honesty, competencies, compassion, or courage.
- Trust does not come automatically with positions of power. Even if it did, trust cannot be sustained by virtue of rank alone.

- In a trust bank account, trust becomes the currency exchanged between people. Dependable behavior is a "deposit," while self-centered and opportunistic conduct is a "withdrawal."

- Low or no trust puts the organization at a competitive and performance disadvantage.

- Trust can be held hostage by a negative emotional reaction; conversely, it can be elevated by a positive emotional response.

- Neuroscientists have discovered that oxytocin, a hormone and neurotransmitter, increases a person's willingness to trust others. When someone is in a safe, nurturing environment, his or her brain releases more oxytocin.

- Trust and collaboration share the same purpose, and without trust any collaboration becomes a farce. People—not processes, policies, strategies, tools, or methods—make up the collaboration, and trust is critical in motivating these people to do the actual work.

- Technical mastery, intelligence, personal and professional drive, past accomplishments, and even vision are admirable and necessary leadership qualities, but they alone do not inspire long-term trust and collaboration. These qualities must be complemented by interpersonal and behavioral competencies.

- In the absence of credible leaders, people will still perform their tasks and abide by organizational rules. They only do so, however, because they want to keep their job, and they perform at the lowest acceptable level possible.

- A collaboration that is built on trust has a deeper meaning and thus has long-lasting power. It energizes, engages, and awakens passion and commitment.

- Influential leaders are not just passive recipients of trust; they are also proactive givers of trust. They view trust as a mutual practice: They work hard to earn and keep it, and they expect and demand others to do the same.

- You cannot pretend to be trustworthy, at least not for a long period. Similarly, you cannot pretend that you trust others, as they, too, cannot fake trustworthiness. Behaviors, particularly during times of stress, will always reveal what you really think and feel.

- The conforming component of the C^4 model relies heavily on the principles of self-awareness: Without self-awareness, a leader has no foundation for developing, sustaining, and modeling trust.

Applying the C^4 Model: Trust (Conforming)

The following questions are intended to initiate self-examination of the trust that exists within your team and organization. Take the time to think about the questions posed here, and be honest with yourself.

- Do you share information (positive or negative) that is helpful to others, or do you withhold it? Similarly, does your team share relevant information? If not, what is keeping all or some of you from practicing transparency?

- Do you treat everyone with kindness, respect, and compassion? Similarly, how do your team members treat each other? What are the social norms in your team?

- Do you follow through on your commitments, even if you do so at considerable personal expense? How do you hold your team to the same level of accountability?

- Explain how you encourage your team members. Do they encourage their followers or associates, and how? What has been the observable result of this encouragement?

- What types of celebrations do you hold for achievements, and what rewards or incentives do you offer for accomplishments? How has your approach helped the performance of the team? How has it helped the team members' perception of you?

- Why do you consider yourself a trustworthy person? Which members of your team display trustworthy behavior? How do you highlight the ideal behaviors of your team members so that others may learn from them or emulate them?

- How healthy is your trust bank account with each member of your team? Name specific behaviors that are deposited into and withdrawn from each bank account. What is your balance in each? Think about some current conflicts within the team, including one that involves you and another team member. How much of this conflict can be traced back to the lack of deposits but constant withdrawals from the trust bank account?

- What emotional reactions does your behavior bring out in your team members? How have these reactions helped or hindered their trust in you? Similarly, what emotions do your team members provoke in you, and how has your trust level been affected?

- Name a collaborative project that has come about as a result of the high level of trust among your team members. How has that inspired more collaboration? Conversely, name a collaborative project that has been derailed as a result of low-level trust among your team members.

- Describe your process for educating your team members about an initiative you are trying to push forward. How do you gain their support? What are the usual reactions you receive? Explain why they are positive or negative.

- How often do you "go it alone" to get things done and make things happen? How does that approach affect you and your team?

Rate your level of openness to trust. As an exercise, ask your team members to rate themselves as well. Use a rating scheme from 1 to 5, with 1 for completely disagree and 5 for completely agree.

- Remains accessible, particularly during a major issue that affects performance (e.g., medical error)   _____

- Seeks to understand others' behavior in the context of their behavioral style and stressors   _____

- Views people as having equal worth, and values differences of opinion   _____

- Allows and encourages others to speak freely   _____

- Manages emotions well to foster open and fear-free communication   _____

- Acts in a manner that is consistent with personal and organizational values   _____

- Holds others accountable for their actions, promises, and decisions   _____

- Invests in and personally supports the development of others   _____

- Recognizes and rewards those who are achieving results, and coaches those who are struggling   _____

- Takes appropriate actions against those who refuse to abide by the team's norms and consciously sabotage team performance   _____

Score yourself:

1–8:   Low level of openness

9–18:   Moderate level of openness

19–25:   High level of openness

References

1. R. Hardin, *Trust and Trustworthiness* (New York: Russell Sage Foundation, 2002, 16).
2. S. Covey, *The Speed of Trust: The One Thing That Changes Everything* (New York: Free Press, 2006, 130–132).
3. G. Stoller, "Doing Business Abroad? Simple Faux Pas Can Sink You," 2007 [http://www.usatoday.com/money/industries/travel/2007-08-23-faux-pas_N.htm]. Accessed December 9, 2010.
4. Deloitte, LLP. "Trust in the Workplace: 2010 Ethics & Workplace Survey," 2010 [http://www.deloitte.com/assets/Dcom-UnitedStates/Local%20Assets/Documents/us_2010_Ethics_and_Workplace_Survey_report_071910.pdf]. Accessed September 13, 2010.
5. M. Delgado, "To Trust or Not to Trust: Ask Oxytocin," *Scientific American*, 2008 [http://www.scientificamerican.com/article.cfm?id=to-trust-or-not-to-trust]. Accessed February 5, 2010.
6. D. Ulrich and N. Smallwood, *Why the Bottom Line Isn't: How to Build Value through People and Organization* (Hoboken, NJ: John Wiley & Sons, 2003, 2–4).
7. W. Bennis and B. Nanus, *Leaders: The Strategies for Taking Charge* (New York: Harper-Collins, 1985, 153).

6

Accountability:
The Soul of Collaboration

*The tools of accountability—data, details,
metrics, measurement, analyses, charts, tests,
assessments, performance evaluations—
are neutral. What matters is their
interpretation, the manner of their use,
and the culture that surrounds them.*

—Rosabeth Moss Kanter, author and professor
at Harvard Business School

Accountability is the obligation to take personal responsibility for one's thoughts, beliefs, words, and actions. Although it often carries a negative connotation, accountability is a neutral competency that enables a person to take ownership of the good and the bad results of her behavior, decisions, and mental models. Accountability is not just about admitting to not delivering on what was promised and then offering fixes for the problem; it is also about paying close attention to the surrounding environment to avoid negative consequences. In this way, accountability is an empowering mental model that puts the person in total control.

Being accountable is necessary in the workplace, and subscribing to the principle of accountability ought to be a requirement for every member of the organization, regardless of title, rank, or employment relationship. For example, the organization should include an accountability criterion in all policies and processes, including employee recruitment and retention, physician privileging and credentialing, all performance appraisals, contract development and review, and vendor selection. The point is that if accountability is a clearly documented and well-communicated expectation, every person who works for and conducts business in the organization is more likely to behave responsibly. The person will perform according to established or agreed-on standards and will think twice about assigning blame to someone else. Accountability, like trust, is a collaboration imperative. If team members choose not to behave according to the standards that promote accountability, dysfunctional relationships develop, performance suffers, and collaboration cannot move forward.

This chapter explores the principle of accountability and its relationship with collaboration. Guidelines for establishing accountability behaviors and assessing the level of accountability within the team are also provided.

The Role of Leaders in Promoting Accountability

In a collaborative culture with an influential leader, accountability is a visible practice. All team members are clear about their specific responsibilities. They are aware of the organization's mission, vision, values, and goals and how they fit into this framework. They are given measures and tools to use in determining if they are moving forward or falling behind on their objectives. They are empowered to do their job, and they are rewarded for their efforts.

Accountability is indispensable in a collaboration because the work is interrelated. For example, if one team member makes an error or falls behind schedule, he must report it to the rest of the team to stem the consequences; failure to disclose a problem in one part could potentially damage the entire work. In addition, taking responsibility for errors is easier in a collaborative setting, where the focus is on correction rather than on blame. Thus, fear of retribution is minimal, if it exists, allowing a more honest exchange among team members.

In a traditional culture with command-and-control leadership, however, the opposite is true. Although management demands and praises the value of accountability, it does not provide the resources and environment that enable accountability. This absence results in widespread confusion, distrust, and underachievement. Influential leaders are aware of these pitfalls and thus behave, and urge others to behave, in a manner that promotes accountability.

Role Modeling

"Leaders lead," as an old saying goes. This is a simplistic view of what leaders actually do; it does not take into account the fact that not everything a leader does is worth following. So let's revise this saying to be more specific: "Leaders lead by modeling good behavior."

Influential leaders are role models of accountability. Their appropriate behavior comes from a conscious choice to live by their conviction, to change harmful mental models, and to manage their emotions. This choice extends to the way they view their enormous responsibility for other people—from the internal senior management team to the governing board to employees to physicians and other clinical providers to the patient population to the community at large. Accountability is a practical instrument that influential leaders use to keep themselves and those around them honest, focused, and productive. Influential leaders know that an organization devoid of accountability is nothing but a collection of people who shift blame, feel victimized, procrastinate, and disguise their incompetence.

One way a leader can role-model accountability is to admit his own mistakes and vulnerabilities in the face of various responsibilities. For example, the leader can share a story in which he "dropped the ball" on an important project. He can explain the steps he took to recover from this event. The story can then be turned into a teaching moment that may inspire others to change their approach to avoid the negative outcome experienced by the storyteller. The point of this exercise, which is called *power of story*, is to show that a lack of accountability has the power to weaken even a strong performer and thus needs to be managed with vigilance.

Another way a leader can role-model accountability is to always, in any challenging situation or conflict, ask: "How did I contribute to this problem?" This simple question must be followed by an actual evaluation of the leader's role, because just posing the question is as good as screaming "I didn't do it!" This show of genuine concern indicates to others that the leader sees herself as accountable not only for the problem but also for the solution.

Stopping the Blame Game

More often than not, when we talk about white-collar crimes (e.g., embezzlement, fraud, Ponzi schemes), we ask: "Who's accountable for this mess?" The question indicates that we have a collective, if unconscious, negative reaction to the word *accountability.*

This perspective extends to the way we approach accountability in organizational life. Historically, and especially in health care, we associate accountability with blame and shame. We regard a director responsible for a certain service line as the "go to"—the person who receives all the complaints and who does all the explaining when a problem emerges in that department. This person, in turn, traces the problem to its origin and then transfers all the ire and miseries to the staff member who committed the actual error, compelling the employee to either resign or take prolonged abuse. An employee who does stay amid this stress feels humiliated, utterly incompetent, fearful of getting fired, and too intimidated to perform the simplest tasks. At this point, the relationship between the director and the employee (and between the employee and the organization) is not just strained; it is broken. And this scenario plays out in front of other members of the department, creating the "us versus them" mind-set among the staff, which decreases their productivity and level of performance. Under the blame scenario, accountability becomes a countdown to doom, where everyone knows it is only a matter of time until the relative peace in the workplace is shattered.

You, as the organizational leader, have the ability to stop the loss of trust and damage to the relationship that this system of accountability perpetuates. Try the following strategies:

1. Analyze the problem for the purpose of preventing recurrence and correcting the error, not for the purpose of shaming the responsible party. Even if this root-cause analysis points to one person, the discussion should remain professional, avoiding name-calling and threats that will trigger an emotional outburst.

2. Provide help and support to the person who is accountable. Retraining, coaching, or shadowing should be considered before firing, sanctioning, or disciplining.

3. Turn around the negative perspective of accountability within the organization by celebrating and rewarding achievements.

4. Clearly communicate the organization's policy of no (or low) tolerance for inappropriate behavior, regardless of who commits it. This behavior includes harassment of the responsible person following an adverse event.

Remember that human behaviors drive or stall execution of processes, policies, and strategies. This concept should be considered when you transform accountability from a fault-finding approach to a fact-finding, rewarding system.

Aligning Values with Behavior

Bad behavior is never acceptable. But this message is often not made clear enough, although it is given plenty of lip service in the organization. For example, leadership may repeatedly and publicly declare that sexual harassment is not tolerated and will be met by serious consequences. However, leadership may look the other way on this issue if the incident involves a high-profile physician or a multimillion-dollar donor. Such a scenario obviously undermines trust, and it also ignores a leader's accountability to others.

When behavior is misaligned with values (personal and organizational), the result is always unfavorable. It is disruptive; it multiplies negative attitudes, such as the sense of entitlement and perception of a double standard; and it promotes rule breaking. It saps energy and enthusiasm, and it causes disengagement.

Influential leaders help their teams align their behavior with values by taking the following steps:

- Regularly reminding the team of organizational mission, vision, and values
- Establishing clear performance and behavioral expectations
- Holding each member accountable to specific performance and behavioral objectives
- Monitoring and measuring performance against standards

Perhaps the most important strategy that influential leaders follow occurs even before problems with misalignment emerge. They are careful with the hiring and recruiting process, selecting candidates whose values best match those of the organization and whose behaviors are most conducive to collaboration.

Confronting Toxic Behavior Immediately

A leader who accepts the accountability mandate undertakes tasks that are unpopular to some but are beneficial to all. Take, for instance, confronting toxic behavior within the team. Even when improper behavior is unseen, it causes as much (if not more) damage as observable behavior. And both kinds of misbehavior diminish the accountability of the people who commit these acts. People who intentionally violate standards, rules, and policies and refuse to participate fully in their work are not interested in taking responsibility for anything. They must be confronted immediately.

Influential leaders are quick responders to toxic behavior. They know that time is a precious resource that cannot be wasted on waiting and seeing what happens or on letting situations work themselves out. Following are the steps influential leaders may take to confront a team member who exhibits toxic behavior:

1. Meet with the individual to discuss the specifics of the problem, including the reasons for the behavior, the consequences for the person, and the effects on others and the work. The leader must firmly state that the misbehavior must stop right away, and possible solutions and resources may be offered. Note that this discussion must be a dialogue, not a monologue, to allow both parties to speak their mind. Seek comments from the individual about every aspect of the situation that is discussed; consider these comments when creating an action plan.

2. Create an action plan with a timetable. This plan specifies the dates of checkup, follow-up, or evaluation with the individual.

3. Observe the individual, and acknowledge positive changes to encourage continued improvement. If the person is slipping back into old, improper behavior, recognize it right away and apply the appropriate consequences.

4. Make team members aware of the individual's change effort to elicit their support.

5. Maintain respect for the individual's dignity, even if the final resolution to the problem is termination.

Highly effective collaboration requires accountability, and accountability is not possible in a toxic environment. The responsibility for eliminating toxic behavior falls squarely on the shoulders of leaders. As Albert Einstein said, "The world is a dangerous place to live; not because of the people who are evil, but because of the people who don't do anything about it."

Being Aware That Lack of Accountability
Leads to Medical Errors

Consider the following recent reports:

> Nearly 2 million patients a year develop infections during their hospitalizations, and 90,000 to 100,000 of them die as a result; hand-hygiene rates range from 30 to 70 percent at most acute care facilities; about 4,000 wrong-site surgeries are performed each year; and the number of sentinel events reported to the Joint Commission rose significantly in five of 10 categories in 2009.[1]

> For fiscal year 2007-08, state health officials in California counted 141 retained foreign objects in patients. For the next fiscal year, 2008-09, the count was 196. And in the first 70 days of the 2010 fiscal year, between July 1 to Sept. 8, 2009, 45 foreign objects had been reported. At this pace, by end of this fiscal year, the number of mistakenly left objects will number 225.[2]

When adverse events such as these occur in hospitals and health systems, the first factors to be examined are the clinical protocols and procedures that providers followed (or did not follow). Discussion of the improper behaviors that led to the breakdown in communication and cooperation among the clinical team becomes an afterthought. In fact, the behavior may be brought up only if it is a clear contributor—for example, when a surgeon walks out of the operating room in the middle of surgery. This approach to evaluating cause and effect is inadequate. Leaders have to understand the behavioral aspects of clinical performance. Consider the following findings:

- The lobbyist group Public Citizen released a report that ranks states' medical boards on the basis of the disciplinary actions they have imposed on low-performing doctors. Medical boards in California, Florida, Minnesota, Maryland, South Carolina, and Wisconsin have consistently placed at the bottom of this ranking,[3] suggesting that in these states poor physician performance is not carefully monitored and thus not met with appropriate interventions. For the complete report, visit www.citizen .org/publications/publicationredirect.cfm?ID=7652.

- A patient safety expert and professor at the Johns Hopkins University School of Medicine wrote a commentary in the *Journal of the American Medical Association* naming both physician arrogance and hospitals' lack of an accountability culture as perpetuating the problem of hospital-acquired infection.[4]

- Leadership expert Warren Bennis and his research team studied doctor-nurse relationships for a prestigious hospital. Their observations started in the operating room, where a "difficult" surgeon was performing a five-hour surgical procedure. Throughout the surgery, the surgeon was irate, rude, demeaning, angry, loud, vulgar, and unreasonably demanding with the nurses and surgical assistants. Bennis and his team were "stunned and puzzled" by this surgeon and the "spiteful obedience" of the nurses and assistants.[5]

In these toxic environments, who do you think are the casualties?

At first glance, it may seem that the culprit of behavioral and accountability lapses is our twenty-first century, fast-paced mindset. We are too busy to think before we act. We are too busy to be accountable for both behavior and technical proficiency. We are too busy saving lives to worry about others' feelings. But note this: The Bennis incident cited above occurred in 1958, not in recent years as with the other two examples. Clearly, we cannot blame bad behavior on our technology-driven way of life.

With all the significant improvements in technology, education, training, universal protocols, critical pathways, and management techniques, it is disturbing that so much preventable patient harm and suffering occurs every single day. This alarming reality warrants a loud call to action, a plea for leaders to practice the principles of influential leadership to enable them to transform their entire culture for the benefit of those who rely on it.

Establishing a Zero-Tolerance Policy

Influential leaders not only confront toxic behavior immediately but also have zero tolerance for deliberate and repetitive misbehaviors. When bad behavior continues after appropriate intervention has taken place and adequate time for correction has passed, the next step is usually termination. At this point, the individual involved is sending a message that she has no intention of conforming to the expectations and demands of the organization. Keeping this person on staff greatly undermines leadership's efforts to create a collaborative, accountable culture. This person also poisons the mind-set of those around her, making it more difficult for leaders to gain employee support and participation.

However, termination should always be the last resort. It is unnecessary in most cases. For example, in my experience, employees who refuse to conform exercise their freedom to leave the organization voluntarily. There are many reasons for this decision, but typically these staff members find that working in an organization that holds them accountable for their own behavior and performance does not match their personal values. They may find that the focus on collaboration, rather than individualism, slows down their climb on the organizational ladder, perhaps incorrectly thinking that collaboration is limiting rather than enriching.

The success of a zero-tolerance policy depends on three factors:

1. *Fairness.* If everyone knows that leadership will terminate those who are unable to conform to an accountable, collaborative culture, the expectation is that the policy will apply to every member of the organization, including leaders and managers. Non-employee physicians are also expected to be disciplined or sanctioned under this policy, which makes the policy fair to everyone and allows it to gain more support.

2. *Consistency.* A leader's behavioral style makes him more or less inclined to practice zero tolerance, causing an inconsistent pattern of practice. For example, an amiable leader may be intimidated by the process and allow bad behavior to continue despite the fact that it creates dysfunction in the team. Worse, this leader will choose interdepartmental transfer over termination, further prolonging and widening the damage to patient care. An interdepartmental transfer policy that does not require fulfillment of a probationary period exacerbates this problem. As a result, poor performers escape accountability simply by moving from one department to another; they modify their behavior for the short term, and then their bad behavior resurfaces in a new unit. The flip side of an amiable leader's nondismissal practice is that of an analytical leader. An analytical leader may be too quick to fire over a minor infraction. This action prevents behavior awareness and correction, and it may cause the organization to lose a highly proficient employee who needs some guidance. Employees will be frustrated by a zero-tolerance policy if it varies from one department to the next.

3. *Training.* All employees who supervise direct reports must be trained on various team strategies, including conflict resolution and holding difficult conversations. Methods learned in such training can be applied on a daily basis, but they are most useful when the zero-tolerance policy must be applied.

When a zero-tolerance policy is fair, consistent, and practiced by trained leaders, it is more likely to earn support than to meet resistance. No one wants to be blindsided anywhere, but particularly in the workplace. Thus, a zero-tolerance policy must be clearly communicated to the entire organization and applied evenly.

One final note about zero tolerance: Leaders breed cynicism among employees when they allow disruptive, irresponsible behaviors to continue. Employees need and want to know that their efforts are being noted. If they see that their leaders are spending more time correcting a bad performer's action than on noticing their achievements, negative attitudes will result. They will begin to resist changes and think that their leaders are playing favorites. Simply, employees want to be treated fairly, and they view a leader's refusal to fire a low performer as unfair.

Practicing zero tolerance is particularly challenging for leaders at lower levels of the organizational chart or new leaders. Unlike senior executives who have the advantage of recruiting and selecting their C-suite team members, lower-level leaders likely inherit their staff and are greatly reluctant to "deselect" them. Worse, these leaders encounter inadequate or inappropriate documentation that would support termination of toxic employees. Ask any frontline manager what he perceives to be the biggest impediment to firing low performers; he will most likely say "human resources."

Accountability and Collaboration

As repeated throughout part II, collaboration enables the achievement of results that are greater than those an individual can attain alone. Accountability, this mental model that empowers a person to take responsibility, enables the collaboration to fulfill its mission and to do its work. A collaboration composed of team members who refuse to be accountable to themselves and to other people will not accomplish anything, such a team cannot be called a collaboration at all and is instead a collection of people with dysfunctional behaviors.

Accountability, like good behavior, is a choice that you can make. You can choose to either take ownership or relinquish control to someone else. The latter is not much of an option, as it leads you to stagnant relationships and career paths. Although being accountable is often the more difficult choice, it presents you with many opportunities for learning and self-development. Accountability also sharpens your behavioral, technical, and interpersonal skills. The choice is obvious.

Collaboration without accountability breeds divergent values and inconsistent work. It is a culture in which the following is seen:

- No one wants to admit to or apologize for their mistakes.
- No one wants to take initiative.
- No one wants to be vulnerable to scrutiny.
- No one wants to compromise or commit.
- No one is empowered to make decisions related to his or her tasks.
- No one wants to make changes for improvement.
- No one wants to do more than is necessary to keep his or her job.

Such a collaboration does not produce excellent results. It produces below-average performance at best and life-threatening outcomes at worst.

So how accountable are your team members? Figure 6-1 is a simple tool for assessing this element. Your answers to these questions will give you a starting point for establishing standard accountability behaviors.

Figure 6-1.   Try This: Assess Your Team's Collaboration and Accountability

Rate each item using this scale: 1 for not at all, 2 for rarely, 3 for sometimes, 4 for often, or 5 for very often.

1. Do members of your team understand what needs to be accomplished, and are they given resources to achieve team objectives? _____

2. Are blame shifting, procrastination, and feeling victimized absent among team members? _____

3. Do members of your team think that their good work is rewarded or celebrated by leadership? _____

4. Do you as a team leader empower your team members to make decisions regarding their assigned responsibilities? _____

5. Does the team use tools to measure and monitor performance? _____

Score yourself:

1–10:   No accountability

11–15:   Inconsistent accountability

16–20:   Above-average accountability

21–25:   High degree of accountability

Establishing Standards of Accountability Behavior

Influential leaders know that they must take the guesswork out of accountability; they must set the direction toward which they want their teams to move so that no one is set up to fail or gets lost in the process. The onus for setting the standards for accountability behavior is on leaders.

Accountability means many things to many people. For some, it entails being the point person—the one who coordinates all the activities and answers all the questions related to a task, project, or service line. For others, it means being the owner of the task, project, or service line—the one who initiates a plan, involves others in its development and execution, makes related decisions, solicits support from and provides resources to others involved, and monitors and maintains it.

Regardless of the depth of accountability, individuals in this capacity must follow standard accountability behaviors. These standard behaviors should be incorporated into performance reviews and other review processes within the organization. Doing so ensures that the standards are being monitored and managed. It also encourages the person's vigilance against misbehavior or attitudes that go against the standards.

Defining accountability behaviors may be difficult at first. One method for initiating this activity is to pick a behavior that everyone agrees is inappropriate or not conducive to accountability. Then, write down opposite terms for that bad behavior and select the term that is the closest opposite. For example, if the selected bad behavior is "finger pointing," the opposite words may be "responsible" and "in charge." Once you have selected the proper behavior to target, write down specific descriptions. Make sure to target the bad behaviors that currently plague the team. Also, consider the following points as you establish these standards:

1. What do you want to accomplish with the standard? More collaboration? Fewer excuses? Fewer errors?

2. Who should participate in creating and approving these standards?

3. How is the standard going to increase collaboration and accountability?

4. Is the standard practical for everyday practice?

5. Is the standard clear?

6. Is the standard transferable to any organizational initiative, or is it too specific to the team, unit, or service line?

7. Do the standards include elements of feedback, celebration, rewards, and maintenance?

8. What consequences should you impose for failure to follow the standards?

9. How will you implement the standards?

Figure 6-2 is a simple representation of a behavior-standard evaluation form that you may use as an example. Such forms may also be used during the hiring process to guide the interviewer in discussing the behavioral expectations in a collaborative culture. The new hire may be asked to sign a behavior-standard agreement.

Accountability and the Conforming Dimension of the C^4 Model

The established accountability behavior is part of the conforming dimension of the C^4 model. This knowledge enables leaders to do the following:

- Identify behaviors that erode accountability and hinder collaboration
- Determine whether the current culture (including processes, policies, and standards) help or hinder these behaviors
- Confront performers who display these negative behaviors, and provide correction plans or decide if termination is the appropriate response

Figure 6-2.   Sample Behavior-Standard Evaluation Form

Performance Standard	Needs Improvement	Successful	Exceptional	Comments/Examples
Respect: Communicates in an open and cooperative manner Avoids gossip and the tendency to spread rumors Avoids the use of demeaning and derogatory remarks Avoids the use of sarcasm	Inconsistently meets one or more of the standards	Maintains confidentiality Consistently complies with organizational policies and practices Appropriately verbalizes concerns and shares information in a constructive manner	Models professional and personal ethical behavior Exemplifies and actively mentors others in behavior that is respectful Willingly discourages disrespectful behavior in co-workers	**Needs improvement:** Counseled on 1/10/10 regarding arguing with the charge nurse on the posted add-on cases for the operating room. Had this discussion in an open forum and was disrespectful in tone and words to a person in a position of authority.

- Set specific behavioral expectations and performance goals for all team members, and evaluate and monitor each member's progress
- Make appropriate resources, such as training, tools, and coaching, available
- Incorporate celebrations and rewards into the culture
- Empower team members to do their job, and encourage them to get involved in decision making and problem solving

The goal of the conforming dimension is to get people (including you, the leader) to behave according to standards that raise the levels of accountability and collaboration. Conforming emphasizes not only the need to be aware of poor behavior but also the need to reward and celebrate good behavior. People are more likely to conform to our standards if their efforts are adequately recognized.

Conclusion

Trust (discussed in chapter 5) and accountability are two sides of the same coin. Both are necessary to create a culture of collaboration that drives peak performance and achieves results that last. Organizational goals, benchmarks, expectations, and strategies are merely guidelines. Your and your team's behavior is what ultimately drives organizational outcomes and determines the organization's success and sustainability. If the mantra of real estate is location, location, location, health care leadership's mantra should be behavior, behavior, behavior.

Toxic behavior has no place in the trust-accountability-collaboration equation. It impedes creativity, innovation, cooperation, and communication. It poisons and disrupts performance, and it stirs up negative energy, making people view their duties as a burden and treat those around them with resentment and contempt.

Influential leaders have zero tolerance for toxic behavior. They choose to focus on developing the skills, talents, and potential of high-level and mid-level performers, and they do not waste time on "curing" the ills of employees who refuse or have no intention to take responsibility for their behavior and performance. Exercising zero tolerance is one way that influential leaders practice their accountability to those they serve. These leaders use good behavior as a competitive advantage, and they expect such behavior from everyone in the organization. As Quint Studer,[6] a transformational leadership expert, states, "Allowing employees with a bad attitude to work in the organization is a morale killer. When leaders begin to hold employees accountable for their attitudes and ask those to leave who do not meet standards of behavior, organizations receive a huge boost."

Finally, the real influencers in your organization are not those who have the best technical skills, have the greatest intelligence, are the most charming, or even hold the highest titles. They are those who consistently hold themselves and other people accountable for performance and behavior.

Key Takeaways

- Accountability is the obligation to take personal responsibility for one's thoughts, beliefs, words, and actions. Although it often carries a negative connotation, accountability is a neutral competency that enables a person to take ownership of the good and the bad results of her behavior, decisions, and mental models.

- If team members choose not to behave according to the standards that promote accountability, dysfunctional relationships develop, performance suffers, and collaboration cannot move forward.

- In a collaborative culture with an influential leader, accountability is a visible practice. All team members are clear about their specific responsibilities. They are aware of the organization's mission, vision, values, and goals and how they fit into this framework. They are given measures and tools to use in determining if they are moving forward or falling behind on their objectives. They are empowered to do their job, and they are rewarded for their efforts.

- Influential leaders are role models of accountability. Their appropriate behavior comes from a conscious choice to live by their conviction, to change harmful mental models, and to manage their emotions.

- Historically, and especially in health care, we associate accountability with blame and shame. Under the blame scenario, accountability becomes a countdown to doom, where everyone knows it is only a matter of time until the relative peace in the workplace is shattered.

- People who intentionally violate standards, rules, and policies and refuse to participate fully in their work are not interested in taking responsibility for anything. They must be confronted immediately.

- Highly effective collaboration requires accountability, and accountability is not possible in a toxic environment.

- Lack of accountability leads to medical errors.

- Influential leaders not only confront toxic behavior immediately but also have zero tolerance for deliberate and repetitive misbehaviors. When bad behavior continues after appropriate intervention has taken place and adequate time for correction has passed, the next step is usually termination.

- When a zero-tolerance policy is fair, consistent, and practiced by trained leaders, it is more likely to earn support than to meet resistance.

- A collaboration composed of team members who refuse to be accountable to themselves and to other people will not accomplish anything, and such a team cannot be called a collaboration at all but instead is a collection of people with dysfunctional behaviors.

- The goal of the conforming dimension of the C^4 model is to get people (including you, the leader) to behave according to standards that raise the levels of accountability and collaboration. Conforming emphasizes not only the need to be aware of poor behavior but also the need to reward and celebrate good behavior.

- Influential leaders have zero tolerance for toxic behavior. They choose to focus on developing the skills, talents, and potential of high-level and mid-level performers, and they do not waste time on "curing" the ills of employees who refuse or have no intention to take responsibility for their behavior and performance.

Applying the C^4 Model: Accountability (Conforming)

The following questions are intended to initiate self-examination of the accountability that exists within your team and organization. Take the time to think about the questions posed here, and be honest with yourself.

- What are the tangible and intangible costs of toxic behavior for your team?

- What behavioral and performance expectations or standards are in place for the team? For the organization as a whole?

- Who among your team members consistently display poor judgment that affects the functioning of the team? What have you done to confront this behavior? Has your response to this bad behavior been effective? Why or why not?

- How do you deal with bad behaviors? How do your team members handle bad behaviors within their own groups?

- Is termination a viable option in your organization? How are terminations and other disciplinary actions handled?

- How do you show your team that their dedication and commitment to excellence are appreciated? How do you encourage them to continue their efforts?

- What is the level of empowerment within your team? Are team members allowed to make decisions regarding their respective responsibilities? Are guidelines in place that team members may follow regarding decisions they are allowed (or not allowed) to make?

- What is the level of blame and blame shifting in your culture? What part does blame play in team conflict or any team challenges? What have you and your team done to resolve these issues? Were your efforts effective? If not, why not?

- Say you are in the middle of a significant event whose solution is being held back by a failure to enact some level of personal or organizational accountability. Based on what you are currently experiencing and the outcome you desire (improved hand-washing compliance, improved core measure outcomes, improved level of quality indicators, for example), what would be your most reasonable response to drive that outcome? Now, what is stopping you from doing it?

References

1. K. Terry, "Do You Hold Staff Accountable for Safety?" *Hospitals & Health Networks*, 2010 [http://www.hhnmag.com/hhnmag_app/jsp/articledisplay.jsp?dcrpath=HHNMAG/Article/data/02FEB2010/1002HHN_FEA_patientsafety&domain=HHNMAG]. Accessed February 17, 2010.

2. C. Clark, "Surgeons Still Forgetting to Remove Objects from Patients," *HealthLeaders Media*, 2010 [http://www.healthleadersmedia.com/content/QUA-245777/Surgeons-Still-Forgetting-To-Remove-Objects-from-Patients.html##]. Accessed February 18, 2010.

3. Public Citizen, "California, Florida Join List of Ten Worst States in Disciplining Doctors; Minnesota Is Overall Worst State while Alaska Is Best," 2009 [http://www.citizen.org/pressroom/pressroomredirect .cfm?ID=2864]. Accessed September 22, 2010.

4. Johns Hopkins Medicine, "Bringing True Accountability to Heath Care: Lessons from Efforts to Reduce Hospital-Acquired Infections," 2010 [http://www.hopkinsmedicine.org/news/media/releases/ bringing_true_accountability_to_health_care_lessons_from_efforts_ to_reduce_hospital_acquired_infections]. Accessed September 15, 2010.

5. C. Pearson and C. Porath, *The Cost of Bad Behavior* (New York: Penguin, 2009, ix).

6. Q. Studer, *Hardwiring Excellence* (Gulf Breeze, FL: Fire Starter Publishing, 2003, 81).

PART
III

What Is Connection?

*Everyone communicates. Few connect. It's difficult to
connect with people while pursuing your selfish agenda.
By nature, connecting is a giving experience.*
—John C. Maxwell, author and leadership expert

The third principle of influential leadership is connection. It is the strategy of influential leaders. Connection is the linkage felt among people who share a similarity, such as the same friends and associates, interests and concerns, careers, status in life, employers, and so on.

Living in the electronic age, in which communication via social media and technological devices has taken the place of much of our daily interactions, we tend to appreciate the value of direct contact more than in the past. Direct contact cannot be replaced or underestimated; it is what builds and strengthens connections. People still want and need to establish relationships, particularly in the workplace, to define or confirm their personal and professional identity and worth. Other people serve as our teachers and students, and they help us grow as human beings.

Connection increases a leader's influence among followers, and this influence in turn spurs followers to do more—improve their behavior, develop their skills and talents, work better and harder, seek and participate in collaborations or teams, and achieve greater results. In a post-recession climate, where every aspect of our professional life seems vulnerable and in a state of flux, a strong connection between leaders and employees is especially necessary. This bond enables the organization to rise above its challenges.

The most important concept to understand is that you cannot lead without connecting. If your leadership is all about targets, efficiencies, and execution, you will not attain successful outcomes. Your employees must first feel inspired, engaged, and connected before they give you their best work. Without a connection with you, your staff will still work, but not as well as needed or desired. Connection really is a distinguishing factor in your leadership strategy.

The good news is that making and sustaining connections can be learned, because connecting is a behavior-based skill. Part III of this book shows you how. Chapter 7 focuses on the various ways leaders connect with followers. Chapter 8 addresses leadership behaviors that kill connections and suggests ways to prevent them.

7

Connection: The Strategy of the Influential Leader

If a leader can't get a message across clearly
and motivate others to act on it,
then having a message doesn't even matter.
—Gilbert Amelio, former CEO of Apple

Methods, tools, technologies, protocols, and systems do not achieve results. People do. It is with people, then, not with processes, that organizational leaders must form a long-lasting connection. This connection is what ultimately determines the success or failure of the leader specifically and the organization as a whole. As mentioned in chapter 1, people will buy into their leaders before they buy into the organization's mission, vision, and values. Staff members who feel a connection with their leaders are engaged, cooperative, collaborative, participative, accountable, passionate about their work, and supportive of change. They are motivated to behave according to established expectations and to perform to the best of their knowledge, skills, and abilities. An organization with such a workforce can dominate any market or industry with consistent, high-quality clinical, financial, and operational outcomes.

The principle of connection validates and puts into practice the concepts of self-awareness and collaboration. Self-awareness enables leaders to *initiate* connections with their employees, while trust and accountability—the imperatives of collaboration— allow leaders to *sustain* these connections. In this way, connection is a strategy that influential leaders use to demonstrate they

159

care for and understand the needs of their employees. A deep connection between the leader and employees raises everyone's level of energy, engagement, motivation, and performance.

In this chapter, the primary ways leaders can connect with their employees are discussed. The four factors—trust, compassion, stability, and hope—that drive people to follow their leaders are described, along with the three behavior-based needs for transforming connections—focus on others, sensitivity, and adaptability.

Are Your Connections Positive or Negative?

Relationships, by their nature, require constant and consistent tending. The quality of the care you put into these relationships translates into either a negative or a positive experience. That is, every one of your interactions is perceived by the other person as good or bad. If you misbehave during a contact, that experience is considered a negative; conversely, if you conduct yourself well, that experience is counted as a positive. This idea is similar to the emotional and trust bank accounts (discussed in chapters 3 and 5) in that connectivity has a cumulative effect: The more your interactions are seen as negative, the less likely you are to develop connections. If you want to increase the positive experiences and thus enhance your connections, you must improve your behavior.

Effects of Negative Interactions

Over time, negative experiences erode the leader's influence. This is particularly true for leaders who give plenty of lip service to forging effective relationships but do nothing to advance that cause. These leaders ignore or do not seek feedback, do not listen to others or share information with them, micromanage their staff, allow their emotions to control them, take accomplishments for granted, and offer more criticism than aid and resources. None of these behaviors is conducive to making and sustaining connections. They breed cynicism, distrust, and resistance to change, even those behaviors that improve organizational functioning. Worse, they can bring productivity to a screeching halt In health care, these repercussions have devastating effects on patient care.

One survey of employees who left their job indicated that 25 percent quit because of "ineffective leadership" and 22 percent resigned as a result of "poor relations" with a manager.[1] While some percentage of turnover is healthy for the organization, to replace the inevitable bad hires, we cannot dismiss the relevance of the findings from attrition studies that claim that failed connections are the primary reason people leave their jobs.

Leadership experts Roger Connors and Tom Smith formulated a guideline for detecting whether a leader's connection with her followers is perceived as negative. This guideline is presented in figure 7-1. According to Connors and Smith, if you agree to three or more of the statements in this guideline, then you are not making a positive connection.[2]

Figure 7-1. Try This: Determine the Quality of Your Connections

---

Rate yourself on each item on a scale from 1 to 10, with 1 being the lowest level of agreement with the statement and 10 being the highest level of agreement.

1. You visibly detect frustration from people during your conversations with them.
2. You note that people begin making excuses before you get into a subject.
3. You hear virtually no positive feedback and receive little encouragement from people in a working relationship with you.
4. You notice that there is lively conversation when things are going well but you get little conversation when things are going poorly.
5. You can tell that people generally try to avoid you.
6. You feel like you always have to search for information as others are reluctant to share information with you.
7. Your conversations with people tend to always focus on what is going wrong and not on what is going right.

Source: Connors and Smith (2009, 23). Reprinted with permission from *How Did That Happen?* published by Penguin Group, copyright © 2009.

Advantages of Positive Connections

Positive interactions strengthen influence. This kind of connection achieves the following:

- Improves performance in all areas
- Boosts morale, quality, and productivity
- Promotes trust and accountability
- Creates a culture in which work is meaningful and its performers are valued

In this environment, the leaders are self-aware and serve as role models of responsible, professional behavior. The employees, in turn, are highly collaborative; they understand what the organization is trying to achieve and how their behavior and performance contribute to that bigger picture. Trust and accountability are not just expected; they are the norm.

Connecting by Following

Influential leaders may connect with others by practicing the principle of followership. Followership is a leader's willingness to listen to those for whom he is responsible so that their wants, needs, and expectations can be fulfilled and the perspectives and information gained can be incorporated into the development or revision of processes, policies, and standards. By paying attention to followers, the leader gains insight and information that he cannot obtain elsewhere. As Peter Drucker said, "Everybody writes books about leadership. Somebody ought to write a book about followership, because for every leader there are a thousand followers." Although followership is an age-old concept and several books have been written about it, its concept is still a novelty in the leadership field.

Following your followers also enables you to make positive connections. You are sending a message that you are interested and invested in what your people experience on a daily basis.

People in general do not follow just anyone or follow out of the goodness of their heart. They need good reasons—a motivation—to follow. And you are responsible for giving them those reasons, but to get to that point you must first make a connection to understand what they want and need. In other words, you have to follow them before they can follow you.

Four Reasons People Follow

In the book *Strengths-Based Leadership*, best-selling author Tom Rath and renowned leadership consultant Barry Conchie explore the results of decades' worth of Gallup research on the topic of leadership relations. Responses from more than 10,000 interviews conducted around the world reveal the four factors that draw people to their leaders:[3]

1. Trust
2. Compassion
3. Stability
4. Hope

Trust

Trust has been discussed extensively in chapter 5, so this factor is not further examined here. However, I cannot overemphasize the significance of trust in forging and sustaining connections and collaborations. But do remember this: Trust in the workplace begins and ends with behavior. One improper behavior can erode the trust exchanged between two people and taint their connection. An accumulation of poor judgments and behavioral missteps will lead to loss of trust, negating the good will and good connection that have been created.

Compassion

Compassion goes beyond empathy. Empathy is a personal understanding of someone else's difficult condition, whereas compassion is a commitment to help that person out of his condition.

Compassion includes kindness, warmth, sensitivity, openness, and tolerance.

Compassion and caring each cannot exist without the other. A leader who genuinely cares about her staff does all she can to provide support, advocacy, and resources. She will not make decisions or issue orders that are harmful to her employees or that sabotage their efforts. She understands that personal lives have a huge impact on professional performance and vice versa, and she encourages everyone in the organization to take advantage of paid time off, break times, employee assistance programs, and other available employment benefits. She is kind and approachable to everyone—from the chairman of the board to the receptionist to the patients' family members—and she always appreciates others' sacrifices and contributions. This leader's compassion is also displayed through the charitable work and funds that she provides on her own and/or through the organization.

People watch what their leader does. If the leader backs up her sentiments with actions, then her followers know that the leader's caring and compassion are real. This recognition, in turn, inspires them to be equally compassionate toward others. In addition, these followers are more likely to support the leader and her initiatives because they know that the leader is their advocate and will pursue only those activities that improve their lives.

A leadership position can easily inflate the ego. Some leaders think they are superior to others by virtue of their rank on the organizational chart. Their decisions and orders do not take into account the safety of employees, the practicality and degree of difficulty of the execution, or the usefulness of the outcomes. Their interactions leave people feeling abused and intimidated. Their attempts to fake compassion become legendary jokes. Employees will talk endlessly among themselves about this leader's sudden display of empathy and caring to manipulate them to do something that benefits only him. No one connects with such a leader.

Stability

To be employed by a financially stable organization will always be a top desire of the workforce all over the world. This kind of stability is a practical need; after all, everyone has to make a living. Research shows that employees who have high confidence in their company's financial future are nine times more likely to be engaged in their job than those who have less confidence in their organization's financial future.[4]

Financial stability, however, is not just based on leadership's ability to grow the business by making wise investments and by closely monitoring its costs and revenues. It is also rooted in leadership's consistent and predictable patterns of behavior. When leaders are honest, accountable, and transparent, they promote confidence among their employees. Employees, in turn, are assured that their leaders are doing what is necessary to keep the organization operational and the workforce working. This is an especially salient feeling during a recession or any other economic crisis. The tacit understanding here is "You do your job well, and we will do our job even better."

Information is a fundamental requirement in a financially stable organization. But information must be collected, analyzed, and shared for it to be useful. Leaders who withhold information (a major misbehavior) create harmful consequences for the organization and the employees. Consider the following example:

> A large hospital hires a consultant to conduct an analysis of its clinical outcomes. The hospital has been experiencing a steady drop in patient quality and satisfaction in each of its departments. The consultant is given a tour of the facility and a chance to speak with employees at all levels. At the end of this rounding, the consultant debriefs the hospital leaders and asks them: "When are you planning to start your first round of layoffs?" The room turns silent as the executives look at each other, waiting for someone else to respond.
>
> The consultant then informs the leaders that while they are busy meeting behind closed doors in an attempt to protect

employees from the eventual bad news, the employees are coming up with their own conclusions. The unstable environment and lack of information have become major distractions. Rumors are rampant, and everyone is stressed. After careful examination of the facts, the consultant determines that the low clinical scores are the direct result of employees being so worried about their job that they commit many mistakes and overlook standard procedures. Layoffs did occur at this organization, but not before the situation affected patient care.

The absence of honesty and transparency (not to mention use of change management strategies) in this example leads to financial, operational, and clinical instability. Although the leaders were concerned for employees and intended to keep up morale by not sharing negative information, they inadvertently caused another problem. This is exactly the type of culture that skilled and talented employees avoid.

Change Management

A leader's first defense against constant change is to manage change. Change makes everyone feel vulnerable, which is why it is generally disliked and avoided. But change management takes away some of these initial reactions, reassuring people that they will come out fine despite the seemingly insurmountable challenge ahead.

Change management is a formal process for enacting change appropriately and effectively. It includes strategies to overcome resistance to change, to explain the need for change to gain buy-in, to update and communicate with those affected by the change, and to implement change in the least disruptive way possible. Leaders who merely tell employees that the organization "must adapt, evolve, or die" and then proceed to work out all the details of the change without communicating with (let alone involving) the employees are not practicing change management. They are inviting conflict and causing a rift in existing relationships.

Hope

Hope and stability are two sides of the same coin. Stability tends to revolve around the present, while hope is oriented toward the future. Leaders who have a positive mind-set about the future and who promote enthusiasm among followers instill hope. Hope, in turn, encourages people to devise a realistic plan and to imagine themselves in more ideal situations. Just like employees do not want to work for leaders who cannot sustain the financial stability of an organization, they do not want to work for leaders who cannot rally them to look beyond their current difficulties.

In *Good to Great*, author Jim Collins writes about the *Stockdale Paradox*. The paradox is named after Admiral James Stockdale, who was captured during the Vietnam War and was a prisoner of war (POW) for more than seven years. Stockdale witnessed many of his fellow POWs die during captivity. Those who died belonged to either the eternal optimist group (those who believed they would be freed immediately) or the eternal pessimist group (those who believed they would never be freed). Stockdale belonged to neither group, but he did cling to hope. He encouraged himself and others to maintain a realistic but hopeful attitude: "We are going to get out of here. It just is not going to be by Christmas. Despite whatever brutal facts we face in the moment, we have unwavering faith that we can and will prevail in the end."[5] The lesson of the Stockdale Paradox is simple: When hope is absent, people lose their confidence and the will to keep trying. When hope is present, people can live through unpleasant or brutal realities and are motivated to make positive and productive choices in preparation for a better future.

Instilling hope, not blind optimism, should be a requirement for all leaders, particularly in health care. Health care employees want to see themselves in a different reality, and they expect their leaders to guide the way there.

Connecting by Sharing Meaningful Experiences

As mentioned earlier, meaningful experiences determine employees' negative or positive perception of the leader. An accumulation of positive experiences will deepen the employee-leader connection, and the opposite is true for negative experiences. The following story exemplifies the concept of sharing meaningful experiences.

Ken Melrose, a senior executive at the Toro Company, the lawnmower manufacturer, had a poor-performing, unionized plant on his hands. The plant was failing to meet acceptable production rates, and the workers did not trust management. Melrose toured the facility and spoke with the plant manager and the head of the union. The union steward said the workforce was upset that the plant manager kept increasing the productivity rate. He argued that the workers could not meet quality objectives at the current increased rate.

Melrose made light of the steward's concerns by suggesting that he and his management team could come into the plant and meet the production rate. To Melrose's surprise, the steward called him out on this challenge. Melrose accepted. Here is how Melrose characterized the ensuing "work" of his management team:[6]

> So here we were all over the plant, about twenty of us, working side by side with the plant people, trying to put these lawn mowers together. There were these buttons that we could hit to stop the line, and they would make a yellow flash. I'll tell you those lights were going off all over the place. It looked like Christmas. The plant manager would yell out, "What's wrong?" and somebody would yell back, "Oh nothing. Management couldn't keep up."

Melrose and his team held a debriefing session after the experience. The team's most amazing discovery was that the plant workers were just like them. They had the same needs, wants, cares, and concerns about life and work. When Melrose went back to the corporate office, he issued this statement: "The next time we need to cut costs or raise the line speed, we're going to do it in a way that values the line workers, because we don't want to lose them and we don't want to fight with them. It's about trusting and valuing and empowering, and having our managers recognize that everyone is important."[7]

This positive experience created a connection between Melrose and his workers. He became the leader the employees wanted to follow because he stood shoulder to shoulder with them and made them *feel* as if they were part of the team. It is an emotional response, which emphasizes a point made in chapter 3 that employees relate to their leaders on an emotional level. Figure 7-2 allows you to apply this emotional-connection concept to your own experience.

When leaders share meaningful experiences with their employees, the level of employee engagement in their work and the support for the leader naturally increase. Employees try harder not only to meet but also to exceed behavioral and performance expectations to show their appreciation that the

Figure 7-2.   Try This: Connect with Others on an Emotional Level

Think about a person (a leader or a subordinate) with whom you enjoy a professional connection. Answer the following questions:

- How does this person behave toward you and others?
- How does this person's behavior inspire or influence your own behavior?
- When did you realize you had a connection with this person? Relate a situation in which this connection was cemented or strengthened.
- What is your emotional reaction to this person's leadership and behavioral style? For example, does this person spend time helping, listening, and offering advice?
- How does your emotional reaction to this person affect your connection with others? Your performance? Your perception of the meaningfulness of your work?
- Do you develop such connections with others?

leader invested time and other resources to find out what they need and recognized their hard work and contributions.

Leadership's Superiority Complex

If we all can acknowledge the truth that developing and maintaining connections and good relationships are crucial to driving performance excellence, then why don't all leaders engage in this practice? The answer to this question requires a genuine self-examination of our prejudices about leader-follower relations. Many leaders do not feel comfortable thinking about, let alone discussing, the superiority mind-set of people who occupy the top tiers of the organizational chart. Thinking this way is a natural and inevitable tendency; it can be observed in all cultures and in all human pursuits. Although it is a painful subject to discuss, the superiority mind-set must be pulled out into the open for the sake of minimizing or eliminating it.

Management's constant finger-pointing at frontline workers is the source of major performance problems, such as apathy, lack of initiative, and lack of motivation.[8] This blaming is just one sign that a leader does not think highly of her employees; they are merely dispensable means to an end. This faulty perception creates a wide gap between the leader and the employees, creating the feeling of isolation and impeding the sharing of meaningful experiences.

Influential leaders are aware of the perils of organizational hierarchy, not just among management but also among physicians. This is why influential leaders work hard to contain their ego, which is the primary source of the inflated sense of self and arrogance. Specifically, influential leaders do the following:

- Respect other people's dignity
- Give credit where it is due, and refuse to take sole credit for anything
- Acknowledge the contribution and hard work of other people

- Refuse to belittle others' job title, experience, training and education, economic status, or personal accomplishments and traits
- Use the word *we* instead of *I*
- Encourage people to give their ideas and opinions, and honor their right to disagree
- Admit their shortcomings, and ask for honest feedback
- Prevent and discourage any form of bullying in the workplace
- Actively seek a personal commonality and professional common ground with other people
- Put the needs of the self behind the needs of others

These practices enable the influential leader to "get over themselves." As a result, influential leaders do not look down on their workforce. Instead, they leverage the skills, talents, and potential of people.

Connecting by Paying Attention

Sigmund Freud, so the story goes, went to his grave perplexed by the question "What do women want?" I wonder if it ever occurred to Freud to simply ask a woman. In health care, puzzled leaders do ask their employees what they want. However, they do little with the answers they get.

Employee attitude, satisfaction, and engagement surveys are indeed useful tools, and the intent behind their administration is admirable. But many of these surveys reveal little useful information. Part of this problem is technical: The questions are not suitable for the purpose or are not clearly worded, the tool itself is unwieldy to use, the participation rate is too low, or the answers cannot be compared to or measured against past results.[9,10] The other part of the problem is behavioral: Even when the survey instrument is effective and the results are fully informative, many leaders do not develop and implement changes or respond to specific comments given. These leaders do give a token acknowledgment of people's participation, but overall their attitude is "Be thankful you have a job."

Much like the attitude that Toro's Ken Melrose demonstrated at the beginning of his experience, many leaders do not take seriously the workplace barriers and emotional burdens their workforce faces. They fail to actively listen to and learn from their people's concerns. Their survey efforts become a way to appease employees or to follow industry standards, not to genuinely improve the working conditions or the quality of employee lives. Here is the simple truth: Employees can tell the difference between those who mean what they do and those who do what they do not mean. This difference is apparent in the way people behave and interact with others, and no amount of regular surveys can convince employees that their leaders care enough about them to pay attention to their problems.

Far too often, employees receive attention only when their performance or behavior causes a problem. The leader then comes to deliver a reprimand or discipline. This kind of attention is unwelcome and unpleasant for both parties, and it conditions employees to think that the only time they have contact with the boss or with management is when something goes wrong. Paying attention should entail much more than this narrow circumstance. It should be done when everything is going great—to reinforce positive behaviors, for example.

So how can leaders pay better attention so that they build a connection with their employees? You may begin with the following strategies:

- Hold listening sessions in which small groups of employees or managers (or both) meet with you to discuss their ideas and concerns. The goal is to receive information, not to defend your position or introduce changes.
- Observe, watch, or shadow employees. The goal is to learn about and witness the daily challenges, not to critique or micromanage the work.

- Ensure that existing policies and standards reflect existing practice and realities. The goal is to eliminate out dated and ineffective approaches, not to create additional processes.
- Be visible on every unit and attend employee events. The goal is to show that you are accessible and approachable, not to assert your importance in the organization.

The Hawthorne Effect

The Hawthorne effect is a behavioral phenomenon discovered by Harvard Business School professors who were conducting environmental-factors research (which lasted from 1927 to 1932) at the Hawthorne Works plant of Western Electric. The professors found that the workers' performance and productivity improved, regardless of the workplace manipulations the researchers introduced (e.g., more light, less light). This finding suggests that the presence of the researchers and their close scrutiny motivated the workers to work faster and better. Although the scientific basis of this research has been challenged in recent years, the evidence at first blush suggests that people do best what their leaders check and inspect.

Three Behavior-Based Needs for Transforming Connections

Making (and sustaining) positive connections with people, much like developing self-awareness, is a deliberate and willful act. It requires a change in behavior and self-examination of what you want to accomplish with the connections you forge. You may want less interpersonal conflict, better performance, fewer miscommunications, greater productivity, fewer turf battles, or more employee participation. These are the actual outcomes that are possible through connecting.

This chapter has presented strategies for forging connections, but before you can apply these approaches you should first learn and adopt the following three behavior-based concepts:

1. Focus on others
2. Sensitivity
3. Adaptability

Focus on Others

Most leaders are so task focused that they forget to be people focused. They forget that they rely on others to get the work done, and if those others are unhappy, the quality of their work declines. A task-focused leader has employees who show up to work only to earn a paycheck. Employees who have a strong work ethic and like their job will put as much of their heart and soul into their activities as they can, for as long as they can. But, eventually, their lack of connection with the leader will negatively affect their morale and motivation. They will leave. Employees who are below-average performers fare even worse in this scenario. Under a task-focused leader, these employees never have a chance to learn new skills or develop their talents. Their poor attitude will worsen and poison the attitude of their co-workers. If they do not leave, they may be terminated. If they are terminated, they may sue.

These difficult scenarios rarely emerge in a culture in which the leader is focused on people—the others. Being focused on others means paying attention to their needs, finding out what they want, minimizing or fully avoiding negative interactions, viewing them as equals (not looking down on them), and sharing meaningful experiences with them. Figure 7-3 presents some principles of focusing on people, not tasks.

Sensitivity

As mentioned earlier, trust, compassion, stability, and hope are found by research to be the four legitimate needs of employees.

Figure 7-3.   The Principles of Focusing on People

- *People are not disposable and replaceable resources.* If you think of your employees as merely the means to an end, you will not make an effort to connect with them.

- *People need leaders, not managers.* "Leadership" connotes guidance and forward movement. "Management," on the other hand, implies control. Which word motivates you more?

- *Success is achieved by people, not by best practices and tools.* The quality of your connections with people dictates the quality of the results they will achieve.

- *People—regardless of job title, salary, education, and skills—have the same needs, wants, and expectations from the workplace and from other people.* A superiority mind-set is divisive and presents a barrier to performance excellence.

Sensitivity is an interwoven thread connecting all of these factors. Sensitivity is the common decency shared by human beings. It is what enables us, regardless of our differing spiritual and political affiliations, to sympathize and empathize with those who suffer misfortunes or to become angry and indignant about cruelty and injustice. It is a critical competency in connecting.

Sensitivity is a tricky behavior to master, because it is demanded by all of our interactions. It presents itself in major moral concerns *and* in minor decisions. Insensitivity is so much easier to commit—sometimes you are being insensitive and do not even realize it. Consider the following story as an example.

Years ago, I had the unfortunate task of firing several people. I conducted the exit interviews on Friday afternoons, because the office would be almost empty then. I wanted to show respect for these employees and provide them with a dignified way of collecting their things without the stares and whispers of a full office. Termination is a difficult experience for everyone involved.

One Friday morning, I sent word to one of the staff nurses to come to my office that afternoon. When she reached my office door that afternoon, she began to sob. In the midst of her tears, she sputtered questions about why she was being fired. She was scared, and I was horrified for having made her feel that way. As soon as I made a connection in my head that it was Friday afternoon in my office and people associated that with firing, I immediately explained to the nurse the reason I called her in.

I showed the nurse a wonderful letter I had received from a patient who was very pleased with her kindness and professionalism. I complimented her and encouraged her to continue her exceptional work so that others could emulate her. She was relieved, and I was apologetic for causing her so much dread and anxiety throughout the day. I had already created a negative experience with this nurse before she sat down in my office. I cannot imagine how much of her fears she shared with her colleagues and how distracted they all were. My hope was that our actual interaction turned her perception around.

The lesson in this true story is this: Be aware of your daily habits and decisions, as they could inadvertently create conditions that are insensitive to others.

Adaptability

Adaptability is the ability to effectively adjust to situations. Adaptable leaders are flexible, quick thinkers and learners, and versatile. They do not get stuck on a method or an approach that does not work, preferring instead to be proactive and resourceful in finding alternatives. Adaptability is an indispensable prerequisite to building connections.

In everyday situations, being adaptable means relating to others according to their behavioral style (see chapter 3). Specifically, the leader must learn how to adjust his communication according to the preference of the person—for example, if a person likes to converse by e-mail rather than face-to-face, or if a person appreciates receiving background information rather than just the main points.

Conclusion

Your success as a leader is inextricably linked to your ability to connect with people. You can connect with followers in a number of ways, but all of the approaches must be characterized by trust, meaning, and caring. Experiences or interactions that are more focused on tasks than on people will be perceived negatively. And these negative experiences accumulate and ultimately erode your connection. Positive experiences, on the other hand, increase your influence and enable you to sustain the connection.

Key Takeaways

- Methods, tools, technologies, protocols, and systems do not achieve results. People do. It is with people, then, not with processes, that organizational leaders must form a long-lasting connection.

- Staff members who feel a connection with their leaders are engaged, cooperative, collaborative, participative, accountable, passionate about their work, and supportive of change.

- Connection is a strategy that influential leaders use to demonstrate they care for and understand the needs of their employees.

- The four factors that drive people to follow their leaders are trust, compassion, stability, and hope.

- The more your interactions are seen as negative, the less likely you are to develop connections. If you want to increase the positive experiences and thus enhance your connections, you must improve your behavior.

- Over time, negative experiences erode the leader's influence. Conversely, positive experiences strengthen influence.

- Following your followers enables you to make positive connections. You are sending a message that you are interested and invested in what your people experience on a daily basis.
- When leaders share meaningful experiences with their employees, the level of employee engagement in their work and the support for the leader naturally increase.
- Learn and adopt three behavior-based concepts to enhance your connections: focus on others, sensitivity, and adaptability.

Applying the C⁴ Model: Connection (Conforming)

The following questions are intended to initiate self-examination of your connection with your team and others who rely on you. Take the time to think about the questions posed here, and be honest with yourself.

- How do you keep your promises and commitments?
- How do you show you care about people around you? How do you find out about their needs, wants, and expectations?
- How do you view your followers? Are you a leader, a follower, or both? Relate a situation in which you learned by following.
- What is the level of connection between you and your employees?
- How often do you visit the units in which real work is done? What have been the benefits of those visits to you? What have been the effects of those visits on employees?
- How well do your followers know you? Do you attend their functions, and do you invite them to your functions? What opportunities exist for you to socialize with and/or get to know your staff?

- What is the level of energy, commitment, and engagement among your employees? Do people take initiative, and are they empowered? Are they supportive of or resistant to change? How do they display ownership of their work?

References

1. R. Connors and T. Smith, *How Did That Happen?* (New York: Penguin, 2009, 24).
2. Connors and Smith, *How Did That Happen?* 23.
3. T. Rath and B. Conchie, *Strengths-Based Leadership: Great Leaders, Teams, and Why People Follow* (New York: Gallup Press, 2008).
4. Ibid, 87.
5. J. Collins, *Good to Great: Why Some Companies Make the Leap . . . and Others Don't* (New York: HarperBusiness, 2001).
6. G. Barna, *Master Leaders* (Nashville, TN: Tyndale Press, 2009, 137).
7. Ibid, 138.
8. A. Gilmore, "Fostering a Passionate Workforce," *Chief Learning Officer*, 2009 [http://clomedia.com/articles/view/fostering_a_passionate_workforce]. Accessed April 24, 2010.
9. G. Klemp and M. Sokol, "How to Make Employee Surveys a Tool for Change," 2002 [http://www.workforce.com/section/09/article/23/24/26.html]. Accessed December 29, 2010.
10. J. Decad, "Employee Feedback Survey Design: Asking the Right Questions," MarketTools blog, 2010 [http://www.markettools.com/blog/employee-feedback-survey-design-asking-right-questions]. Accessed December 29, 2010.

8

Leadership Behaviors That Hinder Connection

Intangibles can become tangible when they are understood and managed, allowing specific leadership actions and choices to define and deliver them on demand.

—Dave Ulrich, author and leadership coach

Influential leaders know that the greatest opportunities for growing an organization lie in maximizing the potential of its people. Studies of American businesses, including health care, reveal the following general truths:

- The average leader spends three-fourths of the workday dealing with people issues.
- People make up the largest single cost in most businesses.
- People are the largest, most valuable asset of any company.
- People are responsible for carrying out (or for failing to carry out) the mission and vision of the organization.

Faced with these truths, influential leaders invest time and effort in connecting with their workforce—that is, building effective relationships that enable the highest levels of performance.

As mentioned in chapter 7, creating and sustaining positive connections with people start with developing the self. Leaders must undertake a comprehensive program of self-awareness, in which they learn about the convictions, mental models, and emotions that power their behavior. Only by being aware can the leader make a choice to act according to behaviors that are most appropriate for inspiring, engaging, and guiding people. You cannot make a connection with others if you are not connected to yourself. That simple truth gets lost in the daily flurry of activity in the workplace.

This chapter closes out the book with a discussion of the mistakes leaders commit. It also reviews the main points addressed in the book.

Even the most conscientious leaders can be blind to habits that serve as barriers to making a connection. Identifying the mistakes described below is the first step toward mitigating their impact on personal and professional performance.

Practicing Command and Control

Leaders are confronted daily by a host of paradoxes. For example, the less time you have to spare, the more you are faced with urgent problems. Similarly, the more you rely on technological advances to do the work, the more people problems you should expect to encounter. Perhaps one of the greatest paradoxes in leadership is this: Leaders gain more power by giving more power. This paradox is at the heart of connection. It reminds us that an influential leader fulfills the primary job of leadership: to lead others in becoming leaders themselves. An authoritarian leader cannot do that.

The conduct of a command-and-control leader is directly opposite that of an influential leader. The command-and-control leader is arrogant, unapproachable, intimidating, emotionally volatile, impatient, judgmental, manipulative, and stingy with praise. His immediate staff and management team, not to mention the rest of the organization, are relieved when he is away from the office. Under his leadership, fear and stress are the ongoing reality. Productivity is high only because he constantly watches and micromanages the work, leaving no opportunities for creativity or innovation. In addition, competition is rampant, pitting team members against one another and introducing toxic behaviors. In this culture, dominating the market and increasing revenues are the main goals. Open communication, cooperative attitudes, and integrated teamwork (the traits of collaboration) are not part of its strategies or operating paradigm.

Is this kind of leader successful? Yes. Is this kind of success sustainable? No. Sooner or later, a command-and-control leader collapses under the weight of unethical behaviors, low staff morale, bad clinical practices, and questionable financial approaches.

Command-and-control leadership is not a behavioral style. Behavioral styles are preferences based on professionalism. Even people with an analytical style are not expected to be rude or manipulative. Command and control, on the other hand, is the product of antiquated, undemocratic mental models.

Refusing to Conduct a Self-Examination

Your behavior is the most critical element in your performance. And you have the full ability to manage you. If you conduct a self-examination, you will learn why and how to transform your daily routine from simply "going through the motions" to "making a difference."

Self-examination takes willingness and courage. It is not an easy exercise to undertake because it has the potential to reveal negative aspects of ourselves that make us uncomfortable or that we may be too busy to deal with or to correct. This kind of attitude, however, only prolongs the status quo—the established approach that no longer works (if it worked at all) in our current reality. There is no bad time to conduct a self-examination, much as there is no bad time to start behaving in a manner that increases your ability to connect with other people.

Self-awareness begins with self-examination. Self-examination (with the help of the C^4 model) helps you identify your mind-sets, habits, emotions, and beliefs and then sort them into "what works" and "what does not work." More important, this in-depth awareness enables you to take consistent, deliberate, and disciplined actions to improve. Essentially, self-examination renews, refreshes, or resets your mind, giving you an opportunity to make better behavioral choices as you go about your day.

Tolerating Damaging Behavior and Attitudes in Yourself and Others

Imagine that you work in an organization in which the following behaviors and attitudes are the norms among leaders:

1. *Self-centeredness.* This is a personal need to be the focus of everything—anywhere, anytime, and for whatever purpose. No one else and nothing else matter, and everyone else has to conform and learn to live with this fact.
2. *Negativity.* This is a cynical, critical, and dismissive mindset. It breeds contempt, and it drains enthusiasm and energy.
3. *Poor communication.* This includes hearing instead of listening, failing to give and get updates and to follow-up and clarify, withholding vital pieces of information, being unapproachable and inaccessible, and speaking in anger or in an accusatory manner.
4. *Passive-aggressiveness.* This is passive resistance to directions, change, initiative, or any other efforts. It is marked by ambiguity, sarcasm, sabotage or obstructionism, sulking, procrastination, and even emotional blackmail.
5. *Lack of acknowledgment.* This is the inability to express praise and gratitude, the failure to give credit when due, the tendency to claim undeserved credit, and the habit of blaming and criticizing.

Unfortunately, far too many people get up and go to work every day in such environments. Fortunately, however, not many individuals who embody all five of these attitudes and behaviors go very far up the organizational ladder without being pulled down a step or two. But highly successful people do exhibit some combination of these habits, thereby limiting the effectiveness of their connections, weakening their influence, and holding their people back.

Do you work in such an environment? Do you tolerate these habits in yourself and in others? If so, why?

Why We Keep These Inappropriate Habits

Why do some people cling to these habits willingly? The following reasons may explain the tendency:

1. *Some people automatically reject change, regardless of how beneficial it may be.* Also called the Semmelweis reflex, this response represents our attachment to entrenched norms, beliefs, paradigms, and behaviors. This reflex is a form of extreme denial that the status quo is a better alternative, and no amount of evidence can prove to us that we are wrong.

The Semmelweis Reflex

As detailed in chapter 2, Ignaz Semmelweis was a tireless advocate of hand-washing practices in hospitals and clinics. At the time—the mid-1850s—physicians and the medical establishment repeatedly rejected Semmelweis's research that showed deaths would decrease or could be prevented by the simple act of doctors washing their hands before and after treating or handling every patient. Although his attempt to convert doctors to his thinking was valiant and lasted until he died, he was ultimately unsuccessful. Semmelweis's recommendation simply ran counter to the prevailing medical knowledge of his day, and he experienced tremendous resistance despite the fact that his argument made sense.

Today, the automatic rejection of any approach, theory, or framework that contradicts well-established and accepted beliefs and practices is called the *Semmelweis reflex*. The Semmelweis reflex is operative in many health care organizations today. It is responsible for the failure to commit to innovation, transform dysfunctional cultures, and improve performance.

---

2. *Some people refuse to accept that these behaviors are negative.* In this case, the existence of these habits is acknowledged, but the idea that they are harmful to others is rejected. The justification is that if a leader has achieved much success in his profession, then his habits may not have been bad after all. Author and executive coach Marshall Goldsmith provides an insightful explanation for this reasoning: "We think our past success is predictive of great things in our future. . . . This wacky delusional belief in our godlike omniscience instills us with confidence, however unearned it might be. It blinds us to the risks and challenges in our work. But our delusions become a serious liability when we need to change. . . . And that's the paradox of success: These beliefs that carried us *here* may be holding us back in our quest to go *there*."[1]

3. *Some people are not ready to change.* Having the *capability* to change and the *willingness* to change are both necessary to transform behavior. It is difficult to persuade people who are not mentally and emotionally prepared for a change. This level of resistance may only be overcome when the person is convinced that the change serves his best interest.

Behavior change is a process—even a lifelong pursuit of study, dedication, and self-discipline. But it must be driven internally by the person, not externally by a third party: The person must make a commitment to his own development.

Failing to Take Advantage of Conflict and Confrontation

Connection does not mean the absence of conflict and confrontation. On the contrary, a culture that embraces collaboration and connection welcomes constructive conflict and confrontation. The operative word here is *constructive*, as this kind of conflict or confrontation is purposeful and helps the team in several ways, such as building commitment, talking candidly about challenges, revealing points of behavioral and performance weakness, and examining solutions and new approaches. But even the constructive type of conflict and confrontation makes the best of us anxious, and we avoid these situations for various reasons, including the following:

1. *Conflict and confrontation force us to be accountable.* The core of a conflict or confrontation within a team is the question: "Are you doing what you promised to do?" This "promise keeping" question (for lack of a better term) is intended to keep the team members honest so that they can maintain focus, take personal responsibility, manage behavior, and achieve their goals. The problems with this question are that (1) no one likes to ask it, and (2) no one likes to be asked it; the question makes people feel judged and pressured.

2. *Conflict and confrontation give us honest feedback.* We are more emboldened during a conflict or a confrontation. Thus, we are not hesitant to speak our mind about the person with whom we are in conflict or about the situation over which we have a problem. This feedback can reveal to us how other people experience us through our behavior and how that experience influences their perception of us. But these revelations can make us feel uncomfortable.

All great relationships require constructive conflict and confrontation to grow and thrive.[2,3] Influential leaders orchestrate the culture in which people can be energized, engaged, and fully aware of their meaningful contributions to the enterprise. Much of the personal and organizational benefits of such a culture can be negated if we fear constructive conflict and confrontation.

Overcoming this fear takes the following steps:

1. *Reconnect with the mission of the organization.* The stated purpose of the organization is to be of service to a great number of people, not to forward one group's interests. When we avoid strategies (like constructive conflict and confrontation) that enable that mission to be fulfilled, we invite not only disruptions but also harm. For example, the collision of two 747 airplanes at the Canary Islands,[4] the explosion of the space shuttle *Challenger,*[5] and countless fatal medical errors occurred because people who knew something was wrong did not speak up. When we reconnect with the primary meaning and purpose of our work, we can gain clarity, courage, and commitment. These ideals then drive us to pursue constructive conflict and confrontation, which help us make better decisions.

2. *View conflict and confrontation as positive rather than negative.* The key is to be intentional and deliberate. Generally, people's mental model about conflict is set to "flight or fight"—that is, we run from it if we cannot fight it. And when we stay to fight, we often (if not always) lose, so we do not bother. This mind-set prevents us from considering a third option: See conflict and confrontation as allies, not as enemies. When our mind regards conflict and confrontation as helpful, we change our emotional reaction and their emotional effects on us.

3. *Get out of the way and let constructive conflict and confrontation do their job.* According to Lencioni, the leader

should enable her people to work out their own problems: "It is key that leaders demonstrate restraint when their people engage in confrontation, and allow resolution to occur naturally, as messy as it can get sometimes."[6] Kerry Patterson and colleagues suggest in their book *Crucial Confrontations* that constructive confrontation is essential to organizational relationships, growth, and prosperity, particularly when it involves people who are at different levels: "We really perked up when the person was about to confront a leader who was more powerful— say a supervisor going head to head with a vice president. And if the person had a reputation for being defensive or even abusive, we couldn't wait to see what happened."[7]

Not Making the Choice to Change

As mentioned repeatedly throughout the book, change—whether personal or organizational—is not easy. It is a journey that takes many years and involves many people. But as the Chinese proverb states, "A journey of a thousand miles begins with the first step."

Despite the clear reasons given in this book and validated by research, behavior change is still a distant goal for many leaders. It is not a decision to which they can make a commitment right away. In fact, some leaders do not even see the need for behavior change. They are convinced that other people are the problem, as if these leaders can manage (let alone lead) without other people. The truth is that no one, regardless of how high performing and high achieving, is immune to poor behavior and poorer judgment. It is easy to give in to toxic behaviors because we are inundated by them every day, but it is hard to erase their effects on our reputation and on the connections we have worked hard to build.

Behavior change should not be treated as an item on your to-do list that gets demoted to tomorrow when you get too busy to deal with it today. If that is the approach you take, you may find that at the end of the quarter your once-deep connection with people has become superficial or your once-robust influence on your staff has diminished. Figure 8-1 suggests ways you can mitigate these effects as well as signal that you are open to making and sustaining connections.

Once you make the choice to change your behavior, do not get discouraged. Use as many tools as possible to help you, and conduct a self-examination before, during, and after your transformation. The good news is that you are most likely already practicing many of the approaches discussed in the book as well as avoiding the pitfalls described in this chapter. Take heart in this fact. Now all you need to do is polish your approach every day to build even stronger connections.

Figure 8-1. Try This: Simple Ways to Invite Connections and Maintain Good Behavior

1. *Do not try to win alone.* Leadership need not be lonely at the top. Build a support team, expand your circle of influencers, and learn to win with others.

2. *Seek immediate feedback.* Do not wait to receive feedback for the purpose of the annual performance review. Pursue feedback actively, especially after an initiative. Such feedback may be casual and verbal, or it may involve a tool such as the Johari or Nohari window. The point is that you must stop, think, and listen about your behavior so that you can understand how it is perceived by others.

3. *Find and become a positive role model.* Study the ways and means of successful influential leaders and compare them to your own. What differences and similarities do you see? Also, make a list of the key attributes of the leader you want to work for, and then ask yourself: "Am I this kind of person?" If the answer is no, then you know what work is ahead of you. Positive role models are all around you; you just have to know the qualities you are seeking.

Conclusion

Because of their achievements, people in leadership positions tend to overestimate their strengths and underestimate their weaknesses. As a result, they often see themselves in a more favorable light than is accurate and fail to gauge their actual impact on those around them. This is a dangerous perspective for leaders because it misleads them to believe that their current approaches work and that their habits do not need improvement.

A leader's behavior is the most important predictor of organizational performance. Everyone watches the leader. Whether the leader likes it or not, she must watch her behavior because it determines whether she can make and sustain connections. These connections, in turn, inspire, motivate, engage, and gain the commitment of followers, who then assume cooperative attitudes and support collaboration. Improper behaviors are an impediment to *sustainable* performance excellence. Technical proficiency, intellect, education, and experience are required qualities of a successful leader. Without consistent and appropriate behavior, however, that leader will not be successful for a long time.

Key Takeaways

- Only by being aware can the leader make a choice to act according to behaviors that are most appropriate for inspiring, engaging, and guiding people.

- One of the greatest paradoxes in leadership is this: Leaders gain more power by giving more power. This paradox is at the heart of connection.

- Your behavior is the most critical element in your performance. And you have the full ability to manage you.

- The automatic rejection of any approach, theory, or framework that contradicts well-established and accepted beliefs and practices is called the Semmelweis reflex.

- Connection does not mean the absence of conflict and confrontation. On the contrary, a culture that embraces collaboration and connection welcomes constructive conflict and confrontation.

- A leader's behavior is the most important predictor of organizational performance. Everyone watches the leader. In turn, she must watch her behavior because it determines whether she can make and sustain connections.

Applying the C^4 Model: Negative Connection (Conforming)

The following questions are intended to initiate self-examination of the behaviors that limit your connection with your team and other people who rely on you. In addition, revisit the "Applying the C^4 Model" sections in parts I and II and reflect on those questions again now that you have completed the book. Take the time to think about the questions posed here, and be honest with yourself.

- What kind of leader are you now? What kind of leader do you want to be?

- How much of your weekly time is spent connecting with others or strengthening those connections? How does that approach benefit your relationships?

- How do you evaluate your own behavior and performance? How do you enable others to evaluate you? What revelations have you learned about yourself, and what actions are you taking as a result of this knowledge?

- What roles do conflict and confrontation play in your team? Relate an instance in which conflict or confrontation led your team to better solutions.

- On a scale of 1 to 5 (1 being not at all and 5 being all the time), estimate the level of these behaviors displayed by you and your team members: self-centeredness, negativity, poor communication, passive-aggressiveness, and lack of acknowledgment. What emotional reactions do these behaviors bring about, and how do they affect the relationships among team members?

References

1. M. Goldsmith, *What Got You Here Won't Get You There* (New York: Hyperion, 2007, 17).
2. Ibid.
3. P. Lencioni, *The Five Dysfunctions of a Team* (San Francisco: Jossey-Bass, 2002).
4. T. Long, "March 27, 1977: The Worst Air Disaster Ever," *Wired*, 2009 [http://www.wired.com/science/discoveries/news/2009/03/dayin tech_0327]. Accessed September 21, 2010.
5. J. Oberg, "7 Myths about the Challenger Shuttle Disaster," 2006 [http://www.msnbc.msn.com/id/11031097]. Accessed September 21, 2010.
6. Lencioni, *The Five Dysfunctions*, 206.
7. K. Patterson, J. Grenny, R. McMillan, and A. Switzler, *Crucial Confrontations: Tools for Talking about Broken Promises, Violated Expectations, and Bad Behavior* (New York: McGraw-Hill, 2004, 6–7).

Epilogue

*Leaders really are the standard setters as far as values
in an organization. The values are the foundation
of behavior within an organization and within the
development of organizational culture, and it is critical
that senior leaders are the champions of values.*

—George Barna with Bill Dallas,
authors of *Master Leaders*

Behavior, behavior, behavior. That is the mantra of influential leadership. Influential leaders are masters of their behavior. This mastery comes from their conscious decision to become self-aware of the values, convictions, mental models, and emotions that drive their thinking, actions, and words. With this wealth of insight, influential leaders are able to identify behaviors that hinder their abilities and negatively affect their relationships and interactions.

Becoming an influential leader requires a complete transformation, and this transformation is not easy. The good news is that it can be done. All one needs is to make a choice between staying the same and making a difference. Influential leaders develop and maintain a culture in which the following are evident:

- Personal and workplace behaviors are aligned with the organizational mission, vision, and values.
- Employees are engaged, energized, and enthusiastic about their work.
- Clear performance and behavioral standards are in place and are followed.

- Toxic behaviors are immediately addressed and not allowed to poison the environment.
- Feedback is sought and received from all levels of employees.
- Collaboration, cooperation, communication, and accountability are expected.
- Achievements are celebrated, rewarded, and acknowledged.
- People, not tasks, are the primary focus.

Many leaders have already invested time and energy into making the transition to become influential. They gain immense satisfaction from this kind of work, and they make a significant difference in the lives of those they serve. I hope this book has given you the tools to make the journey.

I leave you with a final thought from my poem *Born into This World*.

Born into This World

Born into this world come kicking and screaming,
My thoughts are full of wonder and dreaming.
No river too wide, no mountain to tall,
Then someone says, "Don't try, you might fall."

So I learned through life—keep the status quo.
I learned to gripe and wine, singing songs of woe.
It is process and systems that have to change,
All our core metrics are middle range.

Six Sigma, get lean, go do your best.
Try one more program; it's like all the rest.
Performance improvement, we try one by one,
Not one project finished 'till another begun.
Blame shifting victim I was trained to be,
We focused on process, not accountability.

Born into this world come kicking and screaming,
Seeking value and purpose, but work's so demeaning.
Deming, Juran, now Toyota's our savior,
When will we get it, the answer's behavior.

The pain of this journey has helped me to see,
It's put others first and stop thinking of me.
I've learned life is empty not as giver but taker,
To live life with purpose, be a difference maker.

Suggested Readings

Communication and Collaboration

Sheila Embry and Richard Schuttler, "Communication: The Key to Performance," *Chief Learning Officer*, 2009 [http://clomedia.com/articles/view/communication_the_key_to_performance].

Deanna Hartley, "Tips to Improve Workplace Communication," *Talent Management*, 2010 [http://talentmgt.com/talent.php?pt=a&aid=1172].

Talent Management, "Communication, Collaboration Key to Productivity," 2009 [http://www.talentmgt.com/industry_news/2009/October/5067/index.php].

Conflict Resolution

Agatha Gilmore, "Create a Conflict Resolution Culture," *Chief Learning Officer*, 2010 [http://clomedia.com/articles/view/create_a_conflict_resolution_culture].

Culture

M. Barbara Balik and Jack A. Gilbert, *The Heart of Leadership: Inspiration and Practical Guidance for Transforming Your Health Care Organization* (Chicago: Health Forum/AHA Press, 2010).

Chris Edmonds and Bob Glaser, "Culture by Default or by Design?" *Talent Management*, 2010 [http://www.nxtbook.com/nxtbooks/mediatec/tm0110/index.php?startid=36#/38].

Erin Green, "Cultural Savvy Critical for Future Business," *Talent Management*, 2009 [http://www.talentmgt.com/talent.php?pt=a&aid=1097].

John Kotter, "Leading Change: Why Transformation Efforts Fail," *Harvard Business Review*, 2007 [http://hbr.org/2007/01/leading-change/ar/1].

Employee Satisfaction

Michael Fina, "Celebrating Employees: Beyond a Party and a Plaque," *Talent Management*, 2009 [http://www.talentmgt.com/talent.php?pt=a&aid=1105].

Mike Prokopeak, "Don't Kill the Golden Goose," *Chief Learning Officer*, 2009 [http://clomedia.com/articles/view/2766].

Talent Management, "Survey: One in Four Workers Reports Fulfillment in Job," 2010. [http://www.talentmgt.com/industry_news/2010/June/5225/index.php].

Talent Management, "Why the Ongoing Disconnect between Employers and Workers?" 2009 [http://www.talentmgt.com/industry_news/2009/October/5068/index.php].

Chip Wilson, "Don't Control Your Employees; Empower Them," *Talent Management*, 2009 [http://www.talentmgt.com/talent.php?pt=a&aid=1102].

General Management Issues

Ken Blanchard, "The Changing Face of Leadership," *Diversity Executive*, 2010 [http://www.diversity-executive.com/article.php?in=984].

Shelley Hall, "Are You Ready for Change?" *Chief Learning Officer*, 2009 [http://clomedia.com/articles/view/are_you_ready_for_change].

Deanna Hartley, "Can Your Organization Name a CEO Tomorrow?" *Talent Management*, 2010 [http://talentmgt.com/talent.php?pt=a&aid=1322].

Deanna Hartley, "How Managers Can Make or Break Performance," *Talent Management*, 2009 [http://www.talentmgt.com/talent.php?pt=a&aid=1106].

John W. Jones, "Mitigate Employee Deviance," *Talent Management*, 2009 [http://www.talentmgt.com/performance_management/2009/September/1065/index.php].

Steve Lopez, "Eight Tips for Effective Performance Feedback," *Talent Management*, 2010 [http://www.talentmgt.com/talent.php?pt=a&aid=1124].

Joe Santana, "Positive Deviance: The Key to Real Diversity Best Practices," *Diversity Executive*, 2010 [http://www.diversity-executive.com/article.php?in=982].

Talent Management, "Who's Bossing the Bosses?" 2009 [http://www.talentmgt.com/industry_news/2009/August/4989/index.php].

Leadership Development

Chief Learning Officer, "Identifying Executive Skills," 2009 [http://www.clomedia.com/industry_news/2009/August/5011/index.php].

Peter Drucker, "Managing Oneself," *Harvard Business Review*, 2005 [http://hbr.org/2005/01/managing-oneself/ar/1].

Daniel Goleman, "What Makes a Leader?" *Harvard Business Review*, 1998 [2004 reprint] [http://hbr.org/2004/01/what-makes-a-leader/ar/1].

Deanna Hartley, "What's Wrong with the Boss?" *Talent Management*, 2009 [http://www.talentmgt.com/talent.php?pt=a&aid=1108].

Graham Jones, "Real Leadership: The Meaning behind Motivation," *Chief Learning Officer*, 2010 [http://www.nxtbook.com/nxtbooks/mediatec/clo0910/index.php?startid=20#/22].

Michael O'Brien, "What Predicts Executive Success?" *Human Resource Executive*, 2010 [http://www.hreonline.com/HRE/story.jsp?storyId=475354765].

Michael D. Watkins, "The Eight Toughest Transitions for Leaders," *Chief Learning Officer*, 2009 [http://clomedia.com/articles/view/2752].

Self-Awareness

Benjamin Ola Akande and Chuck Feltz, "Why Strategy Fails," *Chief Learning Officer*, 2010 [http://clomedia.com/articles/view/why_strategy_fails].

Trust

Chief Learning Officer, "Trust Me: Credible Leadership Delivers Results," 2010 [http://clomedia.com/articles/view/3643/1].

Craig Mindrum, "Creating a Community Character," *Talent Management*, 2010 [http://www.nxtbook.com/nxtbooks/mediatec/tm0810/index.php?startid=28#/30].

Morey Stettner, *Business Is War: 9 Classic Rules of War for Winning Big in Business* (McLean, VA: National Institute of Business Management, 2001).

Talent Management, "Top Executives Must Rebuild Trust to Lead Companies Out of Recession, Survey Finds," 2009 [http://www.talentmgt.com/industry_news/2009/October/5070/index.php].

Worldatwork.org, "Trust and Ethics in the Workplace Battered by the Recession," 2010 [http://www.worldatwork.org/waw/adimComment?id=40277].

Index

Accountability, 4, 84, 105–106, 135–156
  C⁴ model and, 150–151, 154–155
  change and, 27
  and collaboration, 146–148
  conflict/confrontation and, 187
  connection and, 159
  defined, 135
  as emotions-based employee need, 69
  key takeaways on, 152–154
  role of leaders in promoting, 136–146
  trust and, 116
Advocate South Suburban Hospital (Hazel Crest, Illinois), 101
Agency for Healthcare Research and Quality (AHRQ), 95, 96, 97
Allyn, Stanley C., 87
Amelio, Gilbert, 159
Amiable behavioral style, 73, 74, 93
Analytical behavioral style, 73, 74, 93
Appreciation/recognition, as emotions-based employee needs, 68
Arrington, Eva, 39
Autopilot
  defined, 47
  operating on, 52–53, 56

Barna, George, 195
Beckhard, Richard, 41
"Becoming a High Reliability Organization" (AHRQ), 95
Behavior preference tools, 33–34
Behavioral style
  amiable, 73, 74, 93

analytical, 73, 74, 93
  awareness of others', 110
  communication consistent with, 127
  consistency of, 145
  determining one's, 73–75
  expressive, 73, 74, 93
  impact on communication, 93–94
  as preference, 183
  relating to others', 176
Bennis, Warren, 128, 143
Blaming, 138–139, 170, 184
"Born into This World" (Frisina), 196–197
Brain and behavior, connection between, 52–53, 123–124

C⁴ model
  accountability and, 150–151, 154–155
  collaboration and, 28, 30, 84, 106–107, 110–111
  components of, 28–30
  connection and, 28, 178–179, 192–193
  defined, 27–28
  dimensions of, 15
  self-awareness and, 15, 27–30, 35–37, 56–57, 71–76
  trust and, 126–127, 130–132
  See also Compelling; Conforming; Conviction; Convincing
Center for Studying Health System Change, 92
Challenge/achievement, as emotions-based employee needs, 68

Chamberlain, Lawrence Joshua, 43, 44, 45
Change
    collaboration and, 103
    connection and, 166
    initiating, 24–25
    motivation and, 26–27, 42
    resistance to/rejection of, 40–42, 185–186
    sabotaging of, 27
    self-awareness and, 19
    stages of resistance to, 25–26
    volition and, 42, 54
Charmel, Patrick, 31
Collaboration, 87–113
    building a culture of, 101–106
    C^4 model and, 28, 30, 84, 106–107, 110–111
    conflict/confrontation and, 187
    connection and, 159, 187
    defined, 83–86, 87
    emotional awareness and, 76
    introduction to, 4
    key takeaways on, 108–109
    leadership strength domains and, 33
    as performance improvement strategy, 89–90
    three traits of, 84, 90–100
    See also Accountability; Trust
Collins, Jim, 5, 6, 167
Command/control leadership, 182–183
Communication
    collaboration and, 4, 84, 88, 90, 91–94, 95, 106, 110
    employee engagement and, 70
Compassion, as reason people follow, 163–164
Compelling
    as C^4 model component, 15, 28
    self-awareness and, 42, 54, 59, 71–76
Competition, 83, 84, 88, 98–99, 182–183
Conchie, Barry, 6, 32, 163
Conflict
    accountability and, 145, 155

change management and, 166
    collaboration and, 103, 105, 107, 110–111
    communication and, 92, 94
    connection and, 173, 187–189
    crew resource management and, 96
    emotional awareness and, 60, 76, 77
    self-awareness and, 10, 18
    teams/teamwork and, 97, 99, 100
Conforming
    accountability and, 144, 150–151, 154–155
    as C^4 model component, 28–30
    collaboration and, 84, 106–107, 109, 110–111, 127
    connection and, 178–179, 192–193
    self-awareness and, 88, 127
    trust and, 130–132
Connection, 157–193
    behavior-based needs for transforming, 173–176
    C^4 model and, 28, 178–179, 192–193
    defined, 157–158
    introduction to, 4
    key takeaways on, 177–178
    leadership strength domains and, 33
    by paying attention, 171–173
    positive versus negative, 160–162
    principle of followership and, 162–167
    by sharing meaningful experiences, 168–171
    See also Connection, leadership behaviors that hinder
Connection, leadership behaviors that hinder, 181–193
    behavior/attitudes and, 184–186
    C^4 model and, 192–193
    change and, 189–190
    command/control leadership and, 182–183
    conflict/confrontation and, 187–189

key takeaways on, 191–192
self-examination and, 183–184
Connors, Roger, 161
Conviction
accountability and, 137, 153
as C⁴ model component, 15, 28,
29, 30
collaboration and, 85, 104
emotional awareness and, 75
excellence and, 45
role of, in behavior change, 53
self-awareness and, 39–40, 41,
44, 48–49, 52, 53, 54, 55,
56–57
trust and, 128
Convincing
as C⁴ model component, 15,
28–29, 30
emotional awareness and, 76
role of, in behavior change, 53
self-awareness and, 39, 42, 53,
54, 56–57
Cooper, Robert K., 52, 59
Cooperation, 98–99, 110–111
Covey, Stephen, 63, 106, 117
Crew resource management (CRM),
95–97
Crucial Confrontations (Patterson),
189

Dallas, Bill, 195
Defending, as stage of resisting
change, 26
Deloitte, 119
Denial, as stage of resisting change,
25–26
Diminishing, as stage of resisting
change, 26
Doing the Right Things Right (Joint
Commission), 84
Driver behavioral style, 73, 74, 93
Drucker, Peter, 162

Einstein, Albert, 12, 141–142
Emerson, Ralph Waldo, 47
Emotional bank accounts, 63,
117–119, 160
Emotional control, 64, 103

Emotional intelligence (EI), 60
Emotional triggers, 61–62, 63, 77
Emotions-based employee needs,
68–69
Employee engagement, 68–71
Errichetti, Ann, 101
Every Patient Counts, 96
Excellence, pursuit of, 45, 55
Expressive behavioral style, 73, 74,
93

Feedback
conflict/confrontation and, 187
connection and, 160, 190
employee engagement and, 70
self-awareness and, 20–23, 34,
35, 51
Financial stability, as reason people
follow, 165–166, 167
Followership, 162–167
Fortune magazine, 31
Freud, Sigmund, 171

Gallup research
on leadership relations, 163
on strengths-based leadership,
68
on trust, 69
Gawande, Atul, 85, 96
General Electric, 99
Generational needs in workforce,
66–67
*Get Out of Your Own Way: The
Five Keys to Surpassing
Everyone's Expectations*
(Cooper), 52
Global Challenge for Safer Surgery
Care initiative (World Health
Organization), 96
Goethe, Johann, 21
Goldsmith, Marshall, 21–22, 186
Goleman, Daniel, 17, 60
Good to Great (Collins), 5, 167
Governance Institute, 89–90
Griffin Hospital (Derby, Connecti-
cut), 31
Growth/learning, as emotions-based
employee needs, 69

Hand washing, 40–41, 142, 185
Hardin, Russell, 116
Harris, Rubin, 41
Hawthorne effect, 173
Herzberg, Frederick, 67–68
High-reliability organizations
  (HROs), 95
Hope, as reason people follow, 167
HROs. *See* High-reliability
  organizations (HROs)
Human factors psychology, 90–91

Inclusion/belonging, as emotions-
  based employee needs, 68
Influential leadership
  applying concepts of, 13–14
  four approaches to, 23–24
  introduction to fundamental
    principles of, 1–3
  key takeaways on, 12–13
Ingham, Harry, 22
Institute for Healthcare
  Improvement, 96

Johari/Nohari windows, 22, 190
Joint Commission, The, 84, 91, 96,
  103, 142

Kanter, Rosabeth Moss, 135
Keynes, John Maynard, 1
Kight, Tim, 17
Knowledge workers and employee
  engagement, 70
Kotter, John, 43

Leadership development, 6–7
Leadership Excellence Network,
  99
"Leadership in Healthcare
  Organizations: A Guide to
  Joint Commission Leadership
  Standards" (Governance
  Institute), 89–90
Leadership strength domains,
  32–33, 68
Lencioni, P., 188–189
Listening, 94, 106, 116, 172

Lombardi, Vince, 45
Luft, Joe, 22

Martinuzzi, Bruna, 124
Master Leaders (Barna and Dallas),
  195
Maxwell, John C., 23–24, 157
Mayer, John, 60
Mayo, Will, 102
Mayo Clinic, 101–102, 103
Meaning/purpose, as emotions-
  based employee needs, 69
Melrose, Ken, 168–169
Mental maps/scripts, 10
Mental toughness, 49–52, 55
Motivation, 9, 13, 107, 160
  blaming and, 170
  to change, 26–27, 42, 104
  connection and, 174
  through fear, 45
  generational diversity and, 66–67
  performance and, 5
  self-awareness and, 37
Motivation-Hygiene Theory. *See*
  Two-Factor Theory

Nanus, Burt, 128
NASA (National Aeronautics and
  Space Administration), 95–96
National Center for Healthcare
  Leadership, 99

Patterson, Kerry, 189
Performance
  collaboration and, 89–90, 104
  connection and, 4, 170, 173
  strengths/weaknesses, 103
Performance gap, 5–6
PHT Services Ltd., 96
Power/control, as emotions-based
  employee needs, 69
Power of story, 137
Practicality, 42
Primal Leadership (Goleman), 17
Productivity
  command/control leadership
    and, 182

connection and, 4, 161, 162,
    168–169, 173, 182
emotional intelligence and, 60
Hawthorne effect and, 173
self-awareness and, 3–4, 25, 33,
    42, 56, 60, 68
trust and, 120
Profiles Performance Indicator™
    (Profiles International), 75
Public Citizen, 142–143
Purpose, living with, 43, 45
Purposeful thinking, 47–49, 55

Rath, Tom, 32, 163
Role modeling, 137–138, 190

Safe Surgery 2015, 96–97
Safety
    accountability and, 142–144
    behavior preference tools and,
        33
    behavior strengths and, 31
    best-practice approaches to,
        24–25
    collaboration and, 85
    compassion and, 164
    conflict/confrontation and, 188
    crew resource management and,
        95–96
    effective communication and, 91
    high-reliability organizations
        and, 95
    negative behaviors and, 9
    pursuit of excellence and, 45
    Safe Surgery 2015, 96–97
    TeamSTEPPS® (Team Strategies
        and Tools to Enhance
        Performance and Patient
        Safety), 97
    trust and, 124, 125
Salovey, Peter, 60
Self-awareness, 15–81
    C⁴ model and, 15, 27–30, 35–37
    change and, 19, 24–27
    collaboration and, 88
    components/dimensions of, 15,
        34

connection and, 159
conviction and, 44
definition, 15–16, 17
finding behavior strengths, 31–34
inspiration and, 64
introduction to, 2–4
key takeaways on, 35, 54–56
self-examination and, 19–23
volition and, 39, 41–45
See also Self-awareness, emo-
    tional dimension of; Self-
    awareness, volitional/mental
    dimensions of
Self-awareness, emotional dimen-
    sion of, 15, 34, 59–81
    characteristics of emotionally
        aware leaders, 63–71
    as compelling dimension of C⁴
        model, 71–76, 78–80
    emotional awareness, 60–63
    key takeaways on, 76–78
Self-awareness, volitional/mental
    dimensions of, 34, 39–58
    C⁴ model and, 15, 56–57
    connection between brain and
        behavior, 52–53
    conviction and, 40–41
    key takeaways on, 54–56
    mental dimension, 46–52
    volition, 41–45
Self-discipline, 23, 49–50, 55, 75
Self-examination, 19–23, 34, 35,
    183–184, 192–193
Semmelweis, Ignaz, 39–41, 43, 45,
    185
Semmelweis reflex, 185–186
*7 Habits of Highly Effective People,
    The* (Covey), 63, 106
Smith, Tom, 161
Social/communication styles. *See*
    Behavioral styles
South Carolina Hospital Associa-
    tion, 96
Stepanek, Mattie, 83
Stockdale, James, 167
Stockdale Paradox, 167
Story, power of, 137

Strengths-Based Leadership (Rath
and Conchie), 163
Studer, Quint, 152
Superiority complex, 170–171

Teams/teamwork, 4, 84, 88, 90, 95,
99–100, 110–111
accountability and, 136, 145–148
connection and, 190, 192–193
at Mayo Clinic, 102
mental model of self-awareness
and, 51
toxic behavior and, 140–142,
143–146
trust and, 115–124, 127
values and, 140
TeamSTEPPS® (Team Strategies and
Tools to Enhance Performance
and Patient Safety), 97
"Through Blood and Fire at Gettysburg" (Chamberlain), 44
Toro Company, 168–169
Toxic behavior, 140–142, 143,
144–146, 151–152, 182–183
TRACOM Group, 75
Transparency, 21, 23, 89, 116, 166
Trust, 4, 84, 115–133
C⁴ model and, 126–127, 130–132
connection and, 159, 160, 162,
163
as emotions-based employee
need, 69

key takeaways on, 128–130
performance and, 6
as reason people follow, 163
teams/teamwork and, 115–124,
127
"Trust in the Workplace: 2010
Ethics & Workplace Survey,"
119–120
Two-Factor Theory, 67–68
2010 National Patient Safety Goals
(Joint Commission), 91

Ulrich, Dave, 181
U.S. Department of Defense, 97

Values
accountability and, 139–140
collaboration and, 84
purposeful thinking and, 48–49
self-awareness and, 18–19
strength domains and, 32
Volition. *See* Self-awareness,
volitional/mental dimensions
of

Watson, Thomas J., 15
Wooden, John, 45
World Health Organization, 96

Zero-tolerance policies for toxic
behavior, 145–147